VISIBLE OPS PRIVATE CLOUD

FROM VIRTUALIZATION TO PRIVATE CLOUD IN 4 PRACTICAL STEPS

IT Process Institute

Authors

ANDI MANN
KURT MILNE
JEANNE MORAIN

Visible Ops Private Cloud: From Virtualization to Private Cloud in 4 Practical Steps

First edition published April 2011. Printed in the United States of America.

The Visible Ops series published by the IT Process Institute, Inc includes:

- The Visible Ops Handbook: Implementing ITIL in 4 practical and auditable steps
- Visible Ops Security: Achieving common security and IT operations objectives in 4 practical steps
- Visible Ops Private Cloud: From virtualization to private cloud in 4 practical steps

Credits

Managing Editor: Kurt Milne
Executive Producer: Lakshmi Pedda
Executive Advisor: Scott Alldridge
Project Coordinator: Temple Burke
Copy Editors: Mangione, Payne & Associates
Book Design: Integrity Design and Marketing, Portland, OR

IT Process Institute, Inc.
2896 Crescent Avenue
Suite 104
Eugene, OR 97408
Main Telephone: (541) 485-4051
Main Fax: (541) 485-8163
http://www.itpi.org
info@itpi.org
ISBN: 978-0-9755686-3-7

Acknowledgements

The IT Process Institute extends special thanks to CA Technologies for supporting the development of this book.

CA Technologies is an ongoing supporter of the independent research conducted by the ITPI, and is committed to helping improve the operating maturity and performance of all IT organizations.

ITPI also recognizes a wide range of subject matter experts and supporters whose insight and experience helped shape the content in this book.

Scott Alldridge
Lee A. Ames
Allan T. Andersen
Bryan Ard
Charles Babcock
Charlton Barreto
Matt Bausch
Kevin Behr
Steve Bell
Mark Bowker
Paul Burns
Michael Carper (team)
Debra Cattani
Brian Cinque
Steve Darby
AJ Dennis
Bryan Diehl
John Dodge
Stephen Elliot
Jacqueline W. Foster
Tracy Foy
Mike Gai
Steve Gerick
Birendra Gosai
Mora Gozani
Gordon Haff
Prashanth John
Ramprasad Kan
Joel Kehle
Gene Kim
Bennett S. Klein
Kalyan Kumar
Ubaldo Martinez
Gijo K. Mathew
Tino Mathew
Rich McGinty
Dwayne Meloncon
Vishy Narayan
Michael O'Malley
Mike Orzen
Gregor Petri
Lakshmi Pedda
David Resnic
Matthew T. Richards
Edward J. Roth
Jason Schroedl
Dmitry Shkliarevsky
Ryan Shopp
Cindy Shumacher
George Spafford
Ruben Spruijt
Allen Stewart
Dan Swanson
Jeff Tibbitts
Louis Troise
James Turnbill
Scott Van Den Elzen
Ram Varadarajan
Shyam Verina
Erik Vesneski
N. Vijaykumar
Jeff Weber
Brandon Whichard
Christopher Wraight
David Znidarsic

About the Authors

Andi Mann

Andi Mann has more than 25 years of IT experience across four continents. He has worked in IT for governments, midsize businesses, and global corporations, including Amex, Prudential, and Exxon; in multiple roles with enterprise software vendors such as BMC Software and CA Technologies; and as a leading analyst advising enterprises, governments, and IT vendors ranging from startups to the world's largest companies. Andi is widely published, including in *USA Today*, *New York Times*, *CIO*, *ComputerWorld*, and *TechTarget*. He has presented at numerous industry events, including Gartner ITxpo, VMworld, CA World, Interop, SYS-CON, and SAPPHIRE. Andi blogs at http://PleaseDiscuss.com/AndiMann and on Twitter as @AndiMann.

Kurt Milne

Kurt Milne has more than 20 years of experience in various management, marketing, and engineering positions at leading technology companies, including Hewlett-Packard and BMC Software. His main areas of expertise include IT service management and IT controls, inventory and supply chain management, and computer integrated manufacturing. In his role as managing director of the IT Process Institute, he oversees research, benchmarking, and the development of prescriptive guidance for IT operations, security, and audit professionals. He has led six major research studies about various aspects of IT and data center management. He has written dozens of white papers and articles, and contributed to numerous IT books and publications.

Jeanne Morain

Jeanne Morain is virtualization and cloud expert driving strategic alliances for Flexera Software. Previously, she held various executive roles in marketing, strategic alliance, and product management at such companies as VMware and BMC Software. Jeanne has more than 15 years of experience in systems management, virtualization, and cloud computing, implementing solutions for millions of users across Fortune 2000 companies. She has won numerous awards for her work in business service management (BSM), SaaS, dynamic data center, and virtualization and is a contributing author and co-author of books on BSM, virtualization, and cloud computing. She is a noted industry speaker at such events as VMworld, InterOp, CloudSlam, and SoftSummit. Jeanne blogs at www.universalclient.blogspot.com

Testimonials

"It's not just another picture of architecture or analysis of best practices versus potential pitfalls. It is a *tour de force* description on how to get there. Authors Andi Mann, Kurt Milne, and Jeanne Morain understand what's going to go wrong for those who fail to adopt the right disciplines. They know that virtualization, with its ability to cut and paste servers, both improves resource utilization and magnifies missteps. They forewarn and forearm IT managers for the battle with the forces of disorder they are about to confront."

—CHARLES BABCOCK, EDITOR-AT-LARGE, *INFORMATIONWEEK*

"*Visible Ops Private Cloud* is a tremendous resource for organizations looking to develop and deploy a private cloud. The book's four-phased deployment approach provides a succinct roadmap to implementing a private cloud that is tailored to the unique needs of each business."

—ROGER PILC, GENERAL MANAGER, VIRTUALIZATION & AUTOMATION CSU, CA TECHNOLOGIES

"Andi Mann, Kurt Milne and Jeanne Morain are the experts who share their immense knowledge in this book. The *Visible Ops Private Cloud* is a great book for all IT Professionals who are in the process to plan, build, maintain or optimize their datacenter into a strategic dynamic delivery center. A must read for every IT Pro who is interested in private cloud deployments."

—RUBEN SPRUIJT, TECHNOLOGY OFFICER, PQR, CITRIX TECHNOLOGY PROFESSIONAL (CTP), MICROSOFT MOST VALUABLE PROFESSIONAL (MVP) AND VMWARE VEXPERT

"The infrastructure and architecture aspects of private cloud offer exciting technical challenges. But making users comfortable with renting resources and getting internal IT to shift to a service perspective is the real magic of private cloud success. *Visible Ops Private Cloud* addresses both the technical and human factors that maximize your chance of getting it right the first time."

—STEVE GERICK, CONSULTING IT EXECUTIVE

"Our clients are striving to leverage the benefits of virtualization technology, but are focused on managing the business and operational risks. As is true with all new and changing technology, it is important to have a process to implement as well as sustain the technology in order to realize the value envisioned. The *Visible Ops Private Cloud* book offers practical, specific guidance on how to do just that."

—JEFF WEBER, MANAGING DIRECTOR, PROTIVITI

"Part of private cloud computing's opacity is the mysterious starting point that will best ensure maturation and long-term effectiveness. The clarity of approach and the amount of actionable information in this book keenly indicates the quality of market research ITPI has done on the commonly treacherous practice of virtualization."
—LOUIS TROISE, CONSULTANT

"Virtualization is a great example of the saying, 'With great power comes great responsibility.' Organizations that jump into cloud computing without a solid plan are doomed to firefighting and frustration. This guide outlines the plan that will put enterprise IT on the right path toward private cloud."
—DWAYNE MELANÇON, CISA – PRODUCTS EXECUTIVE, TRIPWIRE, INC.

"The impact of virtualization on our data centers will be comparable to how the steam engine changed the manufacturing sweatshops of the 19th century. Traditional wisdom no longer applied, and new economic laws were introduced. The economic laws on how virtualization will change our IT sweatshops into private clouds are being written as we progress, and the *Visible Ops Private Cloud* handbook is definitely one of the better and more pragmatic examples."
—GREGOR PETRI, CLOUD BLOGGER AND CLOUD ACADEMY FOUNDER

"HCL now has broad experience helping our clients implement cloud solutions spanning public and private clouds. The Visible Ops approach captures many of the lessons we think are key for project success. This handbook offers a solid four-phased approach to implementing a private cloud program."
—KALYAN KUMAR, WORLDWIDE HEAD OF CROSS FUNCTIONAL SERVICES, HCL TECHNOLOGIES LTD – ISD

"The *Visible Ops Private Cloud* handbook both identifies and navigates through the obstacles to implementing a private cloud within the enterprise. It contains a compilation of best practices from top-performing IT organizations that will benefit anyone on their journey to the private cloud."
—JOEL KEHLE, CLOUD ARCHITECT, QUALCOMM

"Like first explorers, IT leaders have been left on their own to find a path to the new world of private cloud. Now, with this book as a guide, private cloud adopters can avoid many of the risks and misadventures experienced by those who went before them."
—PAUL BURNS, PRESIDENT, NEOVISE

"We've helped a broad range of clients with private cloud solutions. The key success factors are increasingly clear. *Visible Ops Private Cloud* lays out a path that can help you learn from the experiences of others and accelerate time to success."
—RAMPRASAD KAN, CHIEF TECHNOLOGIST, WIPRO TECHNOLOGIES

"The authors have done their homework. There are a lot of moving pieces in a private cloud solution. This book condenses a broad range of considerations and recommendations into a simple guide that will help you bring it all together and ensure your private cloud success."
—GEORGE SPAFFORD, AUTHOR, *VISIBLE OPS HANDBOOK*

"ITPI has done it again! Mann, Milne, and Morain have demystified the complexity of virtualization and the private cloud while leveraging the time-tested effectiveness of Visible Ops. IT is in a unique position, providing a bird's-eye view of the flow of value to the customer. This comprehensive work makes the high-risk undertaking of a private cloud initiative accessible to all by providing clear guidance based on a solid methodology. A must-read if your organization is considering a private cloud."
—MIKE ORZEN, CMA, CFPIM, PMP, CO-AUTHOR OF THE SHINGO PRIZE-WINNING BOOK, *LEAN IT: ENABLING AND SUSTAINING YOUR LEAN TRANSFORMATION*

"*Visible Ops Private Cloud* is a worthy addition to the Visible Ops series, taking it to a new level of usefulness and relevance. This much-needed book captures and extends the spirit of the original Vis Ops book by tackling virtualization and cloud computing head on, providing practical methods that make the successful creation and management of competitive private cloud computing environments achievable."
—STEVE DARBY, VICE PRESIDENT OF ENGINEERING, IPSERVICES

"Our customers are often on the fast track deploying private clouds and deciding what role next-generation architectures will play in their data centers. Over the next decade, these technologies will deliver business growth and sustainable competitive advantage. This book lays out a logical and focused approach to optimizing the full potential of virtualization and automation while examining the critical success factors of people, process, and technology."
—STEPHEN ELLIOT, VICE PRESIDENT OF STRATEGY, VIRTUALIZATION & AUTOMATION CSU, CA TECHNOLOGIES

"Cloud computing is changing the way businesses run. This new paradigm shift is centered on cloud computing as the path to new innovation and corporate agility. Cloud requires more than technology and hardware but the ability to understand the impact that it has on process, and most importantly people. The ITPI recognizes what is needed to execute on a successful cloud initiative and has assembled a solid set of recommendations that help focus and manage the journey to the private cloud."
—CARLOS GRANDA, IT SERVICES EXECUTIVE

Executive Summary

Visible Ops Private Cloud presents a four-phased approach for managing the development and rollout of a *private cloud*. It was written with and created for enterprise IT executives and data center managers who are responsible for the success of private cloud initiatives.

The book is based on the study of enterprise IT organizations that have implemented private cloud solutions. It includes ITPI's in-depth analysis of the key competencies these organizations have in common. It is also grounded by the authors' more than 60 years of combined experience in systems management, virtualization, and IT process management.

Private cloud key competencies were identified through surveys and interviews with CIOs, vice presidents of engineering and operations, architects, and IT engineering and operations managers. These IT professionals represent leading technology, financial services, and telecommunications firms, among others. Their private cloud projects range from mid-sized deployments to large-scale private clouds that encompass thousands of servers.

Interest in private cloud is driven by heightened awareness of public cloud offerings that promise instant access to highly scalable computing resources. Enterprise IT is capable of offering private cloud services that deliver access and scalability similar to public clouds.

However, private clouds have three main advantages over public cloud offerings. First, they are tailored to the unique needs of the business. Second, they cost less than external cloud services. Third, they offer better security and greater control of business-critical computing assets.

> Private cloud increases IT agility and responsiveness to better meet the changing needs of the business.

Deploying a private cloud requires segmenting and managing a portion of the data center as a central pool of computing resources. The private cloud infrastructure is highly virtualized and, in many respects, similar to more static consolidated virtual server environments.

With a private cloud, however, IT is built differently, IT is run differently, IT is governed differently, IT is sourced differently, and most importantly, IT is consumed differently.

In a private cloud, there is a high degree of standardization and *automation* that enables low-touch modes of building, deploying, and scaling resources to respond to changing conditions. As a result, cloud services can be provided at lower cost than those delivered by a lower-density static environment. However, the primary value of private cloud is that it increases IT *agility* and responsiveness to meet the changing needs of the business.

Deploying a successful private cloud solution requires solving technical issues related to architecture, infrastructure, and automation. However, success largely depends on getting users comfortable with consuming IT as a service and getting internal IT staff comfortable with designing and delivering IT as a service.

Private cloud initiatives can be managed in parallel with other data center virtualization and consolidation efforts. Both environments leverage high degrees of server, network, and storage virtualization. However, the practices required to manage the more dynamic private cloud environment are considered higher maturity and require higher levels of process standardization and control.

Visible Ops Private Cloud is based on a prescriptive four-phased approach:

Phase 1: **Cut through the cloud clutter**—plan and communicate objectives, manage initial proof of concept efforts, and develop competency roadmaps.

Phase 2: **Design services, not systems**—design business optimized cloud services, enable one-touch service ordering, and implement a repeatable approach for build and deploy.

Phase 3: **Orchestrate and optimize resources**—update monitoring and alerting, deploy a policy engine to codify response and automate resource changes and workload moves.

Phase 4: **Align and accelerate business results**—complete transition to a resource rental model, reshape consumption behavior, and streamline response to changing business needs.

By reading this book, you will be able to:

- Understand the challenges overcome by other IT organizations that have successfully deployed private cloud
- Understand the key people, process, and technology competencies needed for successful deployment
- Follow a four-phased deployment approach to implement a private cloud that is tailored to the unique needs of your business
- Gain acceptance of using a resource rental model by all stakeholders, including internal IT, business users, and management

Whether you are trying to formulate an initial private cloud strategy or refine your current one, *Visible Ops Private Cloud* will help you get it right the first time.

Table of Contents

Introduction

Virtualization has become a mainstream staple of the data center. In the short time since it was introduced, virtualization has significantly improved how critical computing resources are managed. For many IT organizations, limited deployments in test and development environments as well as broader consolidation in production have demonstrated significant and measurable benefits. The benefits, along with increased confidence in service quality, strongly justify broader adoption across the data center.

IT executives are now looking to build on early success and leverage initial investments in people, process, and technology. The two primary approaches for expanding the use and benefits of virtualization are the fully virtualized data center approach and the private cloud approach.

The fully virtualized data center approach includes virtualizing and consolidating servers as much as possible across the data center. It also includes virtualizing other layers of the technology stack, including network and storage, and deploying application or desktop virtualization. The thinking here is that if virtualizing some resources reduces infrastructure and operational costs, then virtualizing more will save even more.

Many organizations that are pursuing this approach now have executive-level initiatives that mandate the extensive use of server virtualization. It's not uncommon to find small, medium, and large IT organizations that are aggressively pursuing server virtualization to extend measured benefits.

The private cloud approach is a variant of the decision to more broadly deploy virtualization. It includes architecting a portion of the data center as a virtualized and highly scalable, shared resource that can be tapped on demand and easily scaled in response to changing usage levels. The thinking here is that virtualization can enable a new service approach to IT consumption—one that lowers costs and increases agility to better meet the needs of the business.

Historically, higher levels of *utilization* of data center assets tend to correspond with reductions in agility. However, automation and *dynamic* management of private cloud resources allow IT to increase utilization and agility simultaneously. Consequently, the benefits of the private cloud approach can exceed those of the fully virtualized approach because private cloud enables higher utilization and operational efficiency.

The private cloud approach also increases the strategic value of IT. By focusing on service agility in addition to cost reduction, IT can respond more quickly to changing business needs. That's because the ability to offer self service access to scalable resources similar to those offered by third-party cloud vendors allows IT to more effectively address fluctuation and diversity in user demand.

There is an emerging consensus about what constitutes a private cloud solution. Characteristics include:

- **Shared**—Pools of server, network, and storage resources are accessed by users from multiple business units.
- **Dynamic**—Resources are tapped on demand, scaled up or down in response to changing conditions, and then retired when no longer used.
- **Self service**—Resources are provisioned on demand through a service catalog.
- **Automated**—Response to service requests, changing resource consumption, and resource or *workload* decommissioning follow *low-touch* workflow routines.
- **Policy driven**—Predetermined rules specify when and where new services are deployed and guide resource changes and workload movement.
- **Metered**—Resource usage may be tracked and reported to users or funders of IT services.
- **Pay per use**—Costs may be billed based internally on resource allocation or even actual usage. Alternatives such as *showback* and other reporting schemes may be deployed instead of true *chargeback*.

Private cloud differs from a fully virtualized data center

A private cloud strategy differs fundamentally from a fully virtualized data center strategy. Your IT organization likely has some form of virtualization in place already. You may be focused on consolidation for test and development deployments or production systems. You also may be leveraging some of the mobility capabilities of the technology for backup, high availability, and disaster recovery in the production environment.

Regardless of how extensive your current use of virtualization is, when you consider virtualization as the foundation for an IT-as-a-Service or Infrastructure-as-a-Service (IaaS) private cloud strategy, you may find:

- **IT is consumed differently.** The consumption of computing resources changes to a "just enough" approach. End users may provision computing resources on demand. Resources may be added or removed (*rightsized*) based on current or expected conditions. Workloads may be moved to other physical hosts (*lift and shift*) to access additional resources. Policies and automation then help harvest resources when they are no longer needed. Overall, a private cloud deployment can change patterns of demand for IT resources.
- **IT is run differently.** Computing resources may be deployed temporarily. IT operations utilize low-touch modes for provisioning and employ more monitoring to detect conditions that warrant *changing resource levels* or moving workloads. A private cloud changes capacity and performance management, tooling, and the use of automation.
- **IT is built differently.** Depending on risk and usage profiles, infrastructure may be designed for normal load instead of peak load. Pooled and shared resources are tapped during transient periods of demand. Servers, network, and storage need to

tapped during transient periods of demand. Servers, network, and storage need to be able to handle movement of large workloads among physical hosts, even among data centers. A private cloud requires a high degree of standardization to facilitate automation and dynamic resource management.

- **IT is governed differently.** Policies must be clarified and codified to determine where, when, and how workloads are provisioned, and then how resources are adjusted. There is less reliance on people fielding requests and making real-time decisions. There is greater use of automation that is driven by rules that determine when to change resources or move workloads. A private cloud breaks down barriers between functional silos and forces highly skilled personnel to develop process, rules, and workflow.
- **IT is sourced differently.** A private cloud forces IT to shift from a technology to a service focus. IT is less focused on provisioning and managing standalone computing resources and more focused on offering and delivering services. In its service-centric role, IT defines and delivers specified, tested, integrated, and ready-to-scale services that are sourced based on policy.

The success of your private cloud initiatives greatly depends on your ability to directly address these differences and plan accordingly.

Private cloud requires more people with amazing kung fu

> *"There are many different architectures and technologies that will promise you the world. But it is not until you move beyond the technology to the task at hand that you realize the need for succinct workflow across functional groups."*
> —DMITRY SHKLIAREVSKY, VICE PRESIDENT OF PROFESSIONAL SERVICES, APPSENSE

Virtualization has the potential to simplify many aspects of managing IT resources, such as provisioning servers, standardizing on golden build images, and increasing workload mobility. Conversely, it has the potential to create issues, such as losing servers, generating nonstandard configurations, and overtaxing staff and skills.

The dynamic nature of virtualization in a private cloud environment makes it easier to do the right things that improve consolidation-driven return on investment (ROI). At the same time, it makes it easier to do the wrong things that increase total cost of ownership (TCO) in production. Forging ahead with broad virtualization deployments without making the right corresponding changes to operations and infrastructure can actually make things worse.

Amazing Kung Fu

Gene Kim, one of the co-authors of the original *Visible Ops Handbook*, has for years kept a list of IT professionals that he calls, "Gene's list of people with amazing kung fu." This list of people who have shown exceptional process engineering awareness fueled a quest that has become the IT Process Institute's overarching mission, that is, to study top-performing IT organizations to find out what makes them different.

The risk introduced by production changes in a virtualized environment is significantly higher than the risk in a physical environment. Consequently, tracking configuration drift, managing approval cycles, and understanding the relationships among servers has become even more critical than in the physical world. Even the smallest change has been known to destroy an entire server farm because servers that were not interconnected previously are now connected by a common physical host. Changes to networks or network attached storage (NAS) can impact entire clusters of host servers. The increased complexity of modern applications and new dependencies has made it more critical than ever to manage change without disrupting service.

Overall, more complexity, more dependencies, more mobility, and more powerful tools for system administrators require more, not fewer basic controls. As a result, you must focus more attention on management practices and process improvements that optimize the utilization of new technology. Bottom line: Virtualization as the foundation for a private cloud increases the need for process controls in production.

More complexity, more dependencies, more mobility, and more powerful tools require more, not fewer basic controls.

Issues and challenges addressed in this book

Virtualization-based private clouds solve some fundamental issues and challenges related to delivering IT-based business services. However, they create other issues that must be addressed if you're pursuing a private cloud strategy.

This book addresses the following issues and challenges:

- **Dynamic nature of virtualization increases complexity and risks**—With virtualization, you can get into trouble much faster because many of the processes and delays that allowed you to catch issues in your legacy environment are no longer in place. For example, in the virtualized environment, it's easy to copy and paste the wrong images, licenses, and solutions into production, resulting in fragile artifacts. Strong processes translate into major upsides from virtualization. Weak processes, on the other hand, will likely result in major delays, issues with security and compliance, and higher costs.
- **Managing agility requires changes to people, processes, and technology**—Current processes, skills, and technologies were designed to manage *static* data centers. The ability to simultaneously increase *workload density* and maintain agility in a private cloud environment will greatly depend on the ability of your

IT organization to shed the traditional static computing approach. Higher levels of standardization and automation are needed to manage dynamic workloads and pools of shared resources.

- **Transformation requires behavior change**—Private cloud solutions bring in additional layers and technologies that require planning and time. However, the primary obstacles to broad adoption aren't the technology, architecture, or infrastructure. Success largely depends on helping users get comfortable consuming IT as a service, and helping the IT staff get comfortable in the role of designing and delivering IT as a service.
- **Demonstrating value means focusing on the business**—Focusing solely on technology or internal IT priorities can doom you to failure. Reducing costs through greater workload density, for example, is great as long as you also enable increased business agility. Whether you strive to reduce provisioning time or quickly scale business applications, your objectives should be to accelerate time to business results. If you don't design private cloud service offerings for the unique needs of your business, then you miss the opportunity to differentiate IT as a preferred service provider. As a result, business executives and application owners may tap third-party providers, jeopardizing the success of your private cloud initiative.
- **Success in the cloud requires an "All-in" approach**—Designing, provisioning, and supporting private cloud services is impossible in a siloed IT organization. Achieving success requires the participation of a cross-functional team. So ensure success by starting with a project team that includes representatives from all functional areas involved in cloud services—server, network, storage, application development, QA and test, support, security, and compliance. When all members focus on their respective areas of expertise and provide input into the larger plan, you break down silos that hinder success in a dynamic service-oriented environment. What's more, you end up with a plan that everyone buys into, and that eliminates finger pointing.

Visible Ops approach—
Common characteristics of top performers

> Visible Ops Private Cloud is based on both quantitative and qualitative analysis of what works.

The IT Process Institute (ITPI) produced this book to help you streamline your deployment of a private cloud. We set out to create a prescriptive set of recommendations that guide the deployment of dynamic virtualized resources in the data center.

We developed our recommendations by studying top-performing IT organizations to discover what factors were critical to the success of their private cloud initiatives. Our research is based on both quantitative and qualitative analysis of what works.

We interviewed over 30 IT executives, infrastructure and operations managers, and virtualization administrators. We asked them about challenges they encountered and key competencies they felt were critical for achieving success with their virtualization-based private cloud initiatives.

These IT professionals represented IT organizations from a wide range of industries. They were predominantly from large enterprise, or enterprise-like IT organizations. They represent a wide range of virtualization maturity ranging from using server virtualization only for HA and DR, to being 90 percent virtualized in production. Those that had made the most progress with their private cloud initiative tended to have high levels of operations and process maturity.

We also used data from ITPI research that identified virtualization management practices that are commonly deployed in static and dynamic resource environments. Those practices have been shown to work across a large sample of companies in a broad range of industries and organization sizes.[1]

We found six key competencies that are common across top-performing IT organizations that have successfully implemented some form of virtualization-based private cloud:

1. **Service-design approach**—Top performers shift from a focus on consolidation to a focus on private cloud services designed to meet the needs of their users. In general, they leverage virtualization to offer better services at lower cost. They specify and certify the infrastructure, and update the process and tools needed to meet service delivery commitments. Then, to drive adoption, they promote the lower cost and better fit of private cloud services as compared to physical or static virtual services. The service-design approach drives broader private cloud adoption by delivering innovative services that address real business needs. It also prevents misaligned virtualization efforts that ultimately result in business users going around IT to obtain services from external service providers.

   By contrast, the fully virtualized data center approach to broader adoption frames virtualization as an internal IT project. One IT executive we spoke with recalled a conversation with her chief financial officer (CFO) who was pushing for consolidation targets. She told him, "You can put a consolidation target on me, but I'm not going to put a target on my group. We are going to focus on superior service delivery to the business in order to drive adoption. If we can't deliver what we promise, then we aren't going to meet the target."

2. **Simplification and standardization**—Top performers simplify and minimize the number of standard configurations for servers and other infrastructure components. They apply significant effort to specification and certification of standard builds and virtualization templates to ensure they meet user, security, and compliance requirements. Specification and certification also help verify that builds meet requirements for efficient production.

   Coupled with a standard-build approach, top-performing organizations also simplify and standardize on a set of *supporting service offerings* such as backup, recovery, and service level commitments. Without exception, top performers publish a list of services, often in the form of a service catalog that highlights what computing resources are available and what supporting services are mandatory or optional. As a result, they take a bill-of-materials mentality in which server builds, templates, and service options are combined to provision a service request. A *loosely coupled* approach to building resources provides flexibility in assembling components to meet a variety of needs. Their focus is on building servers in a way that is fast, scalable, and dead on every time, with almost no variance.

3. **Plan-build-run orientation**—Top performers realize that dynamic resources and workloads in shared *resource pools* cannot be effectively managed with functional silos in place. Many of these top organizations have broken down barriers by adopting a plan-build-run orientation for both organizational structure and process ownership. They use optimized plan efforts to specify and certify various configurations. They use optimized build efforts to ensure that builds are deployed consistently. They use optimized run efforts to help meet service commitments and reduce TCO.

   A plan-build-run orientation also facilitates a well-managed service lifecycle. Top performers identify service owners who are responsible for changes to the service offerings and who assess user value and the cost associated with the offerings.

4. **Shift of highly skilled resources to preproduction work**—Skilled resources are scarce, so applying them early in the lifecycle helps lower TCO. Time and attention upfront specifying, certifying, and documenting helps ensure that everything released into the wild is well designed and well behaved. For example, expending engineering efforts upfront reduces inefficiencies and minimizes operating costs in production.

   The top performers believe that workloads that are built correctly require less work in production. They believe that if people at all stages of the service lifecycle understand workloads better, then they can fix them faster. If not, then scarce, highly skilled virtualization experts spend precious constrained resource troubleshooting. Overall, their goal was to keep the gurus out of the datacenter.

5. **Process-based approach**—We asked IT executives who have mastered private cloud deployments to list the key competencies needed to broadly deploy virtualization. They all answered with some version of, "Focus on process!"

   The top performers told us that they use process to define and refine everyday work. They use process to learn from mistakes and improve efficiencies. They use process as a foundation for automation. They use process to shift work from highly skilled to lower-skilled resources.

   Without exception, the organizations we studied use process to capture knowledge, reduce inefficiencies, and eliminate variations that can drive up TCO. As one IT executive explained, "If you don't start putting processes in place, you're not going to be in business. And why do I say you're not going to be in business? Because you're not going to have a competitive edge. Then all you're doing is building stuff for your competition who is going to end up buying you."

6. **Explicitly documented knowledge**—Top performers capture and share how things are built in systems documentation. They specify how work gets done in run books or process documentation. They also document and communicate policies that guide decisions across the service lifecycle. These clear policies enable the automation of processes related to managing a dynamic environment.

Documentation minimizes reliance on tribal knowledge and *over-the-cubical-wall communication*. A red-book and run-book mentality is critical for managing virtual systems in large organizations.

One IT executive indicated that his organization had grown rapidly through mergers and acquisitions. Virtualization helped accommodate growth. However, reliance on tribal knowledge hampered the merging of smaller IT shops into a larger, more distributed IT organization. To alleviate these "growing pains," the staff thoroughly documented systems, processes, and policies, simplifying and streamlining how systems are built and run.

An overview of the four phases

> "Visible Ops Private Cloud *expands on the concepts of a widely embraced predecessor work, the* Visible Ops Handbook, *and carries them forward into the new demands and risks of a heavily virtualized computing environment. For adopters of ITIL 3, it will feel like a modernization and advancement of disciplines they've already embraced.*"
>
> —CHARLES BABCOCK, EDITOR-AT-LARGE, *INFORMATIONWEEK*

The top-performing organizations we studied use virtualization broadly for private cloud computing. Most, if not all, have realized that things are far more complicated in a virtual environment than in a static resource environment. They consistently report that without improved control, better process management, and systems engineering thinking, virtualization gets in the way of managing shared resource pools and dynamic workloads.

This book focuses on operational procedures and controls that help manage the technology. Our research has uncovered key success factors that we have organized into four implementation phases. Figure 1 illustrates those phases.

We've organized the content around these phases and written the book based on the premise that some practices have dependencies that must be addressed before moving on to the next phase. Overall, the book is intended to be read in order. However, your efforts may include unforeseeable obstacles, problems, and issues that you can only discover along the way. You need to rationalize the guidance in this book in the context of your own private cloud effort.

Our goal is to allow you to learn from the experiences of the world-class IT organizations we have studied. They have already gone where you are planning to go. You can use our findings to educate yourself, your boss, and your team, so you can accelerate your progress toward the private cloud.

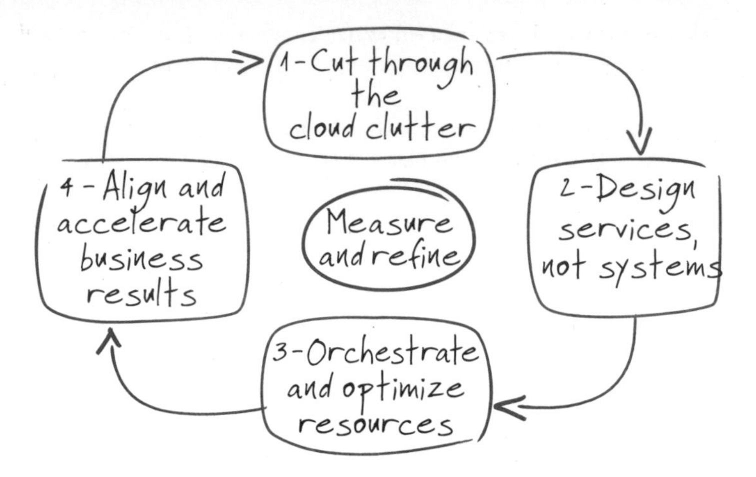

Figure 1. The Visible Ops Private Cloud approach encompasses four phases.

Phase 1: **Cut through the cloud clutter**

The goal of this phase is to refocus your initial virtualization efforts on private cloud deployment. A proof-of-concept (POC) project will help identify challenges and the people, process, and technology competencies required for deploying private cloud resources. Your mantra for these activities is, “Get ready for shared resources and dynamic workloads.”

You will set initial targets for physical, virtual, and private cloud *computing environments*. You will conduct a POC project to begin laying the groundwork for building shared resource pools and managing transitory workloads. We recommend a set of key measures that enable you to compare before-and-after cost, service quality, and agility. With this hard data, you can quantify the improvements achieved in moving to a private cloud environment. You can also build a strong business case for broader deployment and sharpen your focus on achievable implementations based on business needs and requirements. Measures also guide ongoing efforts to refine and improve process and performance.

Phase 2: **Design services, not systems**

The goal of this phase is to meet the specific needs of the business using a service-design approach. The focus is on enabling one-touch ordering of private cloud services. Your mantra for these efforts is, “Simplify the service offering to make sure the right things are built the right way.”

You will use a service-design approach to ensure the private cloud is tailored to the unique needs of your business. You will develop service packages that include supporting services and service level options. You will standardize on a set of configurations and templates to simplify build efforts. You will specify and certify builds to ensure that only fully-tested configurations are released to production. You will enable one-touch ordering from a service catalog that lists available services and bundles. You will also document build information to enable process improvement.

Phase 3: Orchestrate and optimize resources

The goal in this phase is to increase the use of automation to streamline response to changing demand. The focus is on updating infrastructure as well as monitoring and tooling to enable low-touch management of dynamic workloads. Your mantra is, "Automate response to optimize service levels."

You will work to expand the use of automation to standardize and optimize operational processes. You will re-architect the infrastructure to deploy shared resource pools and handle movement of large workloads. You will shift the focus of tooling and monitoring to identify conditions that warrant automated response. You will also deploy initial mobility strategies for backup, recovery, high availability (HA), and disaster recovery (DR). Satisfying user demand for the private cloud services you developed in Phase 2 depends directly on your success in delivering these services in Phase 3.

Phase 4: Align and accelerate business results

The goal in this phase is to complete the transition of IT to preferred provider of *business-optimized services*. The focus is on shifting all appropriate workloads to the private cloud, and shaping demand with a *resource rental model*. Your mantra for this phase is, "Respond to drive business results."

You will move all target workloads to the private cloud to leverage the benefits of the IaaS model. You will measure and communicate the unique mix of cost, service-quality, and agility measures that are representative of each computing environment. You will actively reshape demand for IT resources using a rental model.

The net effect of the final stage of your private cloud deployment will be threefold: The business will see IT as a broker of business-focused, high-value services. The business will view IT as a strategic partner, not just a tactical necessity. The business will consider IT to be a business asset, not just a technology cost center.

Benefits of the Vis Ops approach

> *"What is important now is simply how cost effective and agile your service delivery is. In other words, the clear message is, "IT is not about the computer!"*
> —STEVE DARBY, VICE PRESIDENT OF ENGINEERING, IPSERVICES

What are the benefits of following the recommendations in *Visible Ops Private Cloud*? Based on our study of a wide range of organizations, there are three primary benefits that IT organizations expect from a private cloud deployment.

1 – Agility and responsiveness
2 – Cost reduction
3 – Business alignment

First, IT organizations are looking to break past patterns of behavior and customer expectation that IT is too slow. Historically, IT organizations have a reputation of not moving at business speed. If the business wants something fast, they specifically don't call IT.

Private cloud promises to change that, and shift IT to a more forward leaning and responsive posture. By deploying one-touch service order capabilities, that provision IT services designed to meet specific business needs, and that scale resources automatically to address changing levels of demand—IT can operate at business speed.

Second, in addition to improved agility, private cloud promises to match or exceed the cost effectiveness of either a fully virtualized datacenter strategy, or a public cloud infrastructure as a service provider (IaaS). Higher resource utilization achieved through automated rightsizing of resources, coupled with allocation or use based costing, and a shift to a resource rental model where resources are returned after use—combined can reduce the unit cost of IT below that of virtual static environment. Detailed analysis comparing costs of public and private cloud support for tier 3 and tier 4 applications at companies with revenue over $1B, suggests that private cloud is forty percent lower cost per seat.[2]

Private cloud offers a "Faster, cheaper, better" value proposition for your business!

Several of the IT executives we spoke with that had commissioned detailed internal analysis of their projected cost efficiencies, were confident that their private cloud services were thirty percent lower than public cloud providers offering the same services. At larger enterprises that can spread the fixed costs of automation and tools needed to manage a dynamic environment across a private cloud infrastructure, IT should be able to provision private cloud services at a lower cost than in a fully virtualized and consolidated environment, or in a public cloud service environment.

Third, a private cloud is be based on services designed specifically for your business. Public cloud providers offer generic services that are delivered to hundreds or thousands of customers. You as a private cloud service provider can tailor your services to your business alone. If you choose to follow a service design approach for your private cloud, you have competitive advantage over other service providers.

All together, the private cloud offers a "Faster, cheaper, better" value proposition for your business!

It is not surprising then, that recent surveys of IT executives suggest aggressive plans for widespread adoption. A recent IDC Market Analysis report indicates that one-third of almost 400 IT executives indicated that they expect more than fifty percent of their workloads to be in a private cloud environment by 2013.[3] Said another way, at those companies, more than half of their workloads are targeted for private cloud. That level of enthusiasm really does indicate that IT executives understand the faster-cheaper-better promise of a service oriented private cloud.

Write your own generic success story

How will private cloud benefit your business? Every business is different. Much of the value of a private cloud comes from it being tailored to your business. So it is hard to generalize.

How can you think forward to post-implementation success? Fill in the blanks below to try private cloud on for size at your company.

> Nothing is more important to our business than __________.
>
> Part of IT's role is to help optimize time from idea to business results.
>
> Yet in the past, it could take __ weeks to get IT services set up for ________.
>
> Now it takes ___ minutes.
>
> It's hard to underestimate the value of letting ________ work at their own pace.

Notice, your success story doesn't mention cost? We know every IT shop is on the cost reduction treadmill. Private cloud helps reduce the unit cost of delivering business-aligned services. But that is not the main point. If you promote faster and better to the business, they will expect it to be cheaper as well!

Getting specific about benefits

Specific improvements you can expect from implementing the recommendations outlined in this book:

Improve agility and responsiveness to business needs. A private cloud strategy significantly improves responsiveness and positions IT with a more proactive posture.

- A service-design approach to virtualization adoption and consolidation (Phase 2) is more likely to result in business-aligned services than an approach that emphasizes consolidation.
- Optimized plan-and-build functions (Phase 3) increase the speed of provisioning production-ready resources through one-touch service ordering.
- Enabling self-service provisioning and workflow (Phase 4), similar to external infrastructure as a service (IaaS), Platform as a Service (PaaS), or even Software as a Service (SaaS) providers, helps reduce the need for business users to work around IT to meet their needs. It also allows smaller companies to realize solutions that were previously too expensive or out of reach.

Improve overall quality of service. Broad adoption of virtualization improves overall quality of service.

- Increasing the use of standard configurations and automation (Phase 2) ensures that the build process produces systems that are less likely to fail and easier to fix in production.
- There are also significant benefits from making builds predictable, and reliable, with almost no variance every time. Developers are less likely to hoard resource if they can reliably get want they want when they want it.
- Efforts to improve backup, recovery, HA, and DR procedures (Phase 3) can put more systems under quality control than was previously feasible.
- Leveraging monitoring tools and workload mobility (Phase 4) can ensure automated response to maintain service at levels mandated by service level agreements.
- Overall, virtualized workloads have higher measured application uptime and reduced mean time to resolution (MTTR) as compared to physical environments.[4]

Reduce hardware and facilities costs. Consolidating resources and increasing resource utilization drives down hard computing costs.

- Private cloud resources achieve higher workload density and greater resource utilization than in a static virtualized environment.[5]
- Designing business optimized cloud services (Phase 2) reduces demand for physical and static virtual resources, increasing utilization of cloud resources.[6]
- Implementing architecture optimized for private clouds (Phase 3) increases VM/host ratios, enables additional consolidation of legacy systems, and enhances utilization of IT resources.
- Using shared resource pools for transient workloads (Phase 4) allows optimal consolidation and utilization-driven savings for both hosts and resource pools.[7]

Reduce operating costs and TCO. More effective management of virtualized shared resource pools and mobile workloads improve operating efficiency.

- More controls and simplified service offerings (Phase 2) significantly improve preproduction operational efficiency.[8]
- Optimized service delivery (Phase 3) with standardization and automation can significantly improve the operational efficiency of a wide range of systems maintenance and management functions.[9, 10]
- Low-touch processes for self-service provisioning and workload mobility (Phase 4) drive the highest levels of operational efficiency.[11]

Improve workforce productivity and reduce skills requirements. Getting your most highly-skilled people focused by minimizing distractions increases overall productivity. This also helps push more work to lower-skilled resources who are eager to improve their skills, and allows senior staff to receive the promotions or recognition they deserve.

- Putting your best virtualization experts on process and architectural planning and certification (Phase 2) improves the value-add of top talent.[12]
- Documenting and sharing lessons learned and transferring knowledge to production personnel (Phase 3) along with higher levels of process automation will make everyday work easier.
- Adopting a resource rental model while optimizing low-touch work processes (Phase 4) helps shift overall IT focus away from infrastructure, thereby freeing resources to address higher value-added activities.

Building on the Visible Ops methodology

"For the first time since the Visible Ops Handbook *was written, the vision of push-button golden builds might be able to be realized. Standardizing on small, medium, and larger server configurations while specifying and certifying templates for different environmental, performance, security, and compliance requirements is HUGE. I don't think it can be overemphasized how hard this is to do in the physical world, and how easy in virtual."*

—SCOTT VAN DEN ELZEN, SENIOR SYSTEMS ARCHITECT, IP SERVICES

Your success in implementing the practices outlined in this book depends, in part, on following the prescription found in the *Visible Ops Handbook*. Before you think we are shamelessly plugging a previous book and flip to the next chapter, let us explain.

Written in 2004, the *Visible Ops Handbook* has sold more than 130,000 copies. The Visible Ops methodology continues to be recognized as powerful approach to minimizing the hair-on-fire style of managing the data center.

The extensive use of virtualization as a foundation for shared resource pools and dynamic management practices in a private cloud environment make the advice in the *Visible Ops Handbook* more relevant than ever.

If you deploy a private cloud without a foundation of proven operational controls, you are asking for trouble. The attitude of "we are too dynamic to control what we do" is a recipe for pain.

In a private cloud environment, the Visible Ops prescription is more relevant than ever.

A foundation of change, configuration, and release practices and processes is really a starting point for broad virtualization and private cloud deployment. If you can't effectively manage core data center processes in a physical and static environment, you are likely to experience significant issues managing them in a virtual and dynamic environment.

Summary of Visible Ops concepts

Those who have read the *Visible Ops Handbook* are often struck by how compressed the key concepts are in the book. It lays out a memorable and prescriptive course of action that enables IT to gain real working control of the data center. This summary of key concepts from the book can help drive the success of your private cloud project:

- **Stabilize the patient.** Focus on systems that create the greatest amount of firefighting. To stop self-inflicted wounds, reduce or eliminate access, document a change policy, notify stakeholders, use change windows, and reinforce the process.

- **Electrify the fence.** Managing change on the honor system doesn't work. Put a fence around critical systems and electrify the fence to create a trust-but-verify preventative control.
- **Modify first response.** Integrate change and incident management to reduce MTTR. Look at approved and detected changes as a first step in diagnosing the cause. If needed, expand the circle by including changes made in the last 72 hours.
- **Create a change team.** Form a change advisory board with relevant stakeholders. Track requests through authorization, implementation, and verification processes.
- **Implement a catch-and-release project.** "Bag and tag" all assets in the data center. For each asset, figure out what is running on it, what services depend on it, who has responsibility for it, and how fragile it is.
- **Find fragile artifacts.** Mark each fragile artifact with a do-not-touch sign and avoid changes to it. Work systematically to replace fragile artifacts with standard builds.
- **Prevent configuration mutation.** Avoid making changes and freeze configurations during the catch-and-release project.
- **Create a release team.** Move the most senior staff members away from firefighting and assign them to build the mechanisms that deploy systems into production.
- **Create a repeatable build process.** Design a process to produce golden builds in a predictable and repeatable fashion. Golden builds go through specification and certification before deployment into production.
- **Rebuild instead of repair.** If the build process is repeatable and production configurations don't drive from golden builds, consider rebuilding instead of repairing to restore service.
- **Implement a Definitive Software Library (DSL).** Make the release team responsible for generating builds that are stored instead of for provisioning production. Make the operations team responsible for deployment into production.
- **Create a production acceptance process.** Reduce instances in which release and production teams undermine each other's work. A successful acceptance process allows both teams to focus on business problems despite their slightly different objectives.
- **Define a production plan for patch-and-release refresh.** Patch ideally belongs in the release management process. Strive to apply test patches on preproduction systems before moving to production.
- **Close the loop between preproduction and production.** All production changes must be reflected in new builds. When systems are rebuilt, they will be replaced with functionally identical systems.

These core practices apply to physical, virtual, and private cloud environments. If you are deploying virtualization and private cloud in an operating environment that doesn't have strong change, configuration, and release practices in place, you should adopt at least some of the framework of operational controls that we recommend in the *Visible Ops Handbook*.

Key differences for private cloud

Several key Visible Ops concepts take on a new level of focus in a private cloud:

- In a physical static environment, change is something to control or even minimize. In a private cloud, change is triggered on purpose in response to anticipated conditions. Change is a strategy used to increase workload density and simultaneously optimize utilization and agility.
- Virtualization makes it much easier to implement changes in the data center. In a private cloud, it is more important to electrify the fence and prevent unauthorized changes than in a physical environment.
- Virtualization makes implementation of a golden-build strategy and a repeatable build process possible. However, it also makes it easier to tweak standard builds or overlook the need to update the library of stored builds, thereby creating unwanted fragile artifacts.
- Managing a *server as a fuse* and following a rebuild instead of repair process is now easier with virtualization than in a physical environment. If a workload can be created with one-touch provisioning, then that same workload can be rebuilt from scratch in response to a service outage. Or a working image can be stored on network storage and a critical application can quickly be restored on the same or a different host server.
- Managing a *server as a library book* is a new concept in *Visible Ops Private Cloud.* Checking computing resources in and out as needed is an effective way to increase utilization rates. Managing a resource rental model is a key component of a dynamic resource management strategy.

Mapping the application lifecycle

The *Visible Ops Handbook* follows a specific path that begins in production and then moves upstream. Phase 1 focuses on optimizing production operations functions, stabilizing the patient, and modifying first response. In Phase 2, the path moves upstream to improve build functions by tagging and replacing fragile artifacts. In Phase 3, it continues even further upstream in the software development lifecycle to optimizing planning practices and establishing a repeatable build library. Phase 4 brings in measurement to enable continuous process improvement.

As Figure 2 illustrates, the *Visible Ops Handbook* follows a run-build-plan sequence, while *Visible Ops Private Cloud* moves in the opposite direction, using a plan-build-run sequence.

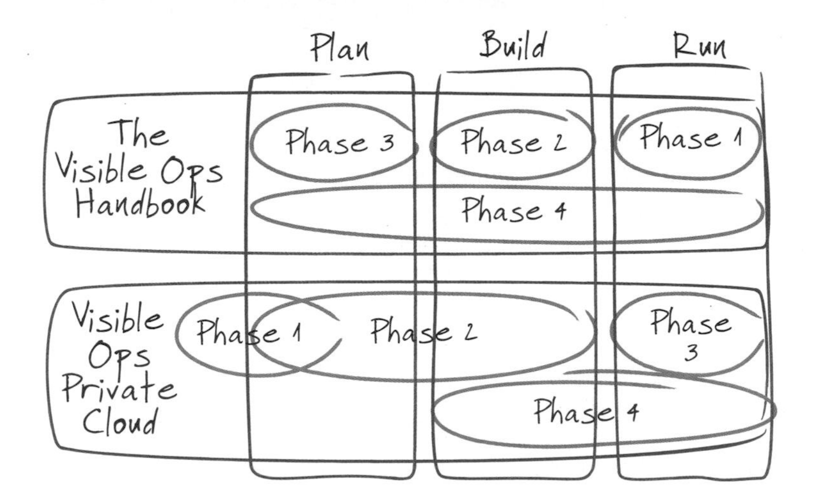

Figure 2. While the Visible Ops Handbook *moves upstream in the application lifecycle,* Visible Ops Private Cloud *moves in the opposite direction.*

In *Visible Ops Private Cloud* we assume that the following types of basic controls are in place before you start a private cloud deployment:

- You've clamped down on unplanned changes in production.
- You've removed or minimized one-off systems that are hard to upgrade and support in production.
- You've established some form of repeatable build library to specify and build standard configurations to minimize variance and improve supportability.

Phase 1: Cut through the cloud clutter

"Without the right set of processes, procedures, and planning, technology can open the business up to new risks. By creating a project team to discover, design, operationalize, and manage our strategic initiatives in this area, we ensure that we protect our company while enhancing overall competitive agility."
—JEFFREY D. TIBBITTS, CIO WINDSOR MARKETING GROUP

What are you going to do?

Your goal in this phase is to build on your current virtualization efforts, using them as a launch pad for private cloud. Regardless of how extensively you are using virtualization now, the way you consume, run, build, and govern that portion of your infrastructure that you set up as a private cloud will be different. Focus your efforts in this phase on thinking ahead to identify and prepare for things that will likely change as you deploy higher levels of automation. Your mantra for this phase is, "Get ready for shared resources and dynamic workloads."

Being aware of the outcomes you want to achieve from a private cloud deployment helps you focus your efforts and break down barriers across multiple functional areas within IT. By building people, process, and technology competencies early, you can reduce risk and ensure that you effectively manage the more dynamic cloud environment.

If you treat private cloud as an enterprise strategy instead of as a series of projects, you'll experience fewer of the false starts that tend to erode the cost and agility benefits of virtualization and reduce the chances of a successful private cloud deployment. As you develop your goals and objectives, take time to learn from your mistakes as well as from the successes (and missteps) of others.

Issues and indicators

In this phase, we address the following issues:

Issue	*Narrative Example*
Virtualization introduces new critical points of failure.	"Our private cloud strategy includes changing resource levels for business-critical applications when they are needed most. There are more dependencies and more critical points of failure. There's no room for error. Last week, a simple right click to change the number of CPUs brought down the host and 15 servers. Changing the logical unit numbers on our SAN disabled our carefully planned and tested backup procedure."
Virtualization requires more experts with a systems view and multiple areas of expertise.	"Even when we hire people with what seem to be the right skill sets, they often don't have the broad experience needed to architect a private cloud. Virtualization makes it easier to build servers but harder to figure out systems-level issues. Our silo mentality makes everyone a specialist. It's difficult to find generalists who understand the broad spectrum required to create good architectures."

Issue	*Narrative Example*
Virtual sprawl creates configuration drift and higher operating expenses.	"Private cloud is all about embracing change as a strategy to increase agility and utilization. But virtualization has set us back on change management rigor. We had a solid change process, but virtualization made it easy to copy, cut, and paste a server, tweak it, and send it out. So we started making changes outside of our process. All of a sudden, every server is a snowflake that looks just a little different from the others."
A dynamic environment without adequate controls is a recipe for pain.	"With virtualization we get into trouble faster. Manual processes and lack of communication among operational groups have resulted in configurations that are unsecure, faulty, or loaded with risks that impact the user experience. In fact, one of our admins cut and pasted the wrong image. It contained a full license of the CRM application. We couldn't prove that all users weren't accessing the app. That little oversight cost the company $6 million in unexpected software license costs during the year-end audit."
All fruit is not low hanging.	"We tried to put all our workloads in the private cloud. We didn't take the time to identify good targets for each environment. As a result, we wasted a lot of effort on things that shouldn't have been virtualized."
Routine maintenance causes unnecessary compliance issues.	"We were hit with compliance failures because we moved an electronic medical records application to a host that wasn't at the required patch level. We were trying to minimize downtime due to planned maintenance. How were we supposed to know what the host patch level should be? I didn't even know the app was in scope for compliance."
Virtual machines are harder to discover.	"Discovery doesn't work if the virtual machine is off. We've had numerous applications disappear and then later be double counted because we couldn't find them."
Utilization is being reduced by *zombie virtual machines*.	"In some cases, we've replaced underutilized physical servers with underutilized virtual servers. We are afraid to consolidate more VMs onto the host because of performance issues. We don't know who the application owners are. Some workloads are rarely used. Others haven't been touched since the week they were created."
Poor performance is causing business users to lose confidence in IT.	"In some cases, we didn't understand the memory or I/O resource requirements for workloads. Too many heavily utilized applications on the same host led to big performance hits for the business. We were focused on how much money we were saving with consolidation, but we forgot to assess the user impact. We lost momentum due to low business confidence."
Monitoring and reporting don't provide the data we need to optimize utilization.	"Capacity wasn't an issue when servers were underutilized. Now we need historical performance data for CPU, memory, I/O, and storage IOPS to determine how to mix workloads and optimize utilization. We have to have visibility to enable automated response to changing conditions."
IT is struggling to meet (SLAs).	"We now have multiple VMs with different SLAs on the same host. It's not clear how to manage resources on the host. Poor capacity visibility, poor planning, and pairing of different applications with different SLAs make every performance issue a potential fire drill."
Current change and configuration process doesn't accommodate the dynamic nature of virtualization.	"We moved 20 servers to a different host to keep services running during maintenance. The change team wanted us to submit 20 change tickets. They don't get it. Now it's our job to collect the data needed to prove that type of change is low risk, and better discern between low-risk and high-risk operational changes."

How are you going to do it?

The goal in this phase is to build on current virtualization efforts, using them as a launch pad for private cloud. The actions that help achieve results include:

1. Put together a plan to get to private cloud. To create a solid plan, you'll need to shift to a portfolio view of the infrastructure that includes physical, static virtual, and private cloud resources; set initial private cloud goals and objectives; and identify basic characteristics of different computing environments.
2. Identify baseline measures to highlight differences in cost, service level, and agility for each environment. Hard data helps you communicate results and justify broader adoption based on real performance.
3. Start a POC project to build skills and scope changes that will be required as you shift from a focus on virtual to a focus on the more dynamic private cloud environment.
4. Gain insight into your applications so you can target workloads to the appropriate computing environment. This involves taking an inventory of tier-1, -2, and -3 applications and their attributes, and using that inventory to identify the optimal computing environment for each application.
5. Clean up the current environment to minimize unnecessary work. Use your inventory data to identify workloads that are the best fit for physical, virtual, and private cloud environments.
6. Create competency checklists for people, process, and technology to guide private cloud efforts. You will expand these competencies as you move into Phases 2, 3, and 4.

Set computing environment objectives

> *"IT organizations should start with the destination in mind when they are building out their design for operationalizing IT as a service. Solid architectures start from creating a service-centric design around key business requirements. Large enterprises will have unique challenges around scale and will have to determine what technologies or group of technologies will work based on their unique business factors."*
>
> —BRYAN DIEHL, SENIOR MANAGER, LARGE TELECOMMUNICATIONS PROVIDER

If your organization is like most, your initial virtualization efforts have fueled success and momentum, and delivered consolidation-related benefits. Now you want to leverage your virtualization investment and move beyond the focus on cost benefits. Private cloud does promise to further reduce unit-level infrastructure and operating costs. But more importantly, it promises to increase agility to meet changing business requirements.

If you have the luxury of starting from scratch, you might build a private cloud in a greenfield data center. This "data center of the future" approach can provide a focused way to prove concepts, build skills, and master key competencies. It's more likely, however, that you'll build out a private cloud in an existing virtualized portion of the data center.

In either case, to effectively deploy a private cloud, you need a plan.

Adopt an infrastructure portfolio view

The first step in planning a private cloud is to adopt a portfolio view of the infrastructure. Your portfolio encompasses three or four computing environments: physical, virtual, private cloud, and, optionally, *hybrid cloud*.

Figure 3 shows how measures can help you identify the basic value proposition for each environment in the portfolio. Each environment has different cost, agility, service-quality, and footprint profiles. You can build a model of your infrastructure with initial targets for footprint or the number of applications that will be in each.

	Physical	Virtual	Private Cloud	Public or Hybrid Cloud
Unit cost	$$$	$$	$	$ or $$
Agility	-	--	---	??
Service quality	*	**	***	??
Footprint	%	%%	%%%	%

Figure 3. Metrics help understand the basic value proposition for each computing environment.

Although hybrid and *public clouds* are beyond the scope of this book, you can include them in your portfolio to help establish a case for or against using public cloud IaaS.

Each computing environment has different attributes that determine which types of workloads it best accommodates. You can use estimates to set cursory targets that highlight the projected size and scope of the private cloud portion of your infrastructure.

Many of the IT executives we interviewed planned to put 30 to 50 percent of workloads in their private cloud environment. The January 2011 IDC cloud survey of almost 400 IT executives from midsize and enterprise IT organizations found similar intent. About one-third of respondents believed that 50 percent or more of their workloads will be supported in a private cloud environment.[13]

Set initial goals and objectives

Private cloud represents a shift to business-optimized IT services and also a rental (or utility) model for IT resources. A library-book approach to finite-duration deployments can minimize the tendency to overprovision resources, thereby reducing overall demand. It also optimizes resource utilization by increasing workload density while maintaining overflow capacity that is shared by multiple hosts.

Private cloud offers lower annual unit costs of IT, including lower capital expense (cap-ex) achieved by maintaining higher workload density. It offers lower operating expense (op-ex) through increased standardization and automation that results in reduced IT management effort. It offers equal or better service levels with mobility features used to prevent service outages and to better respond to incidents. Perhaps the greatest benefit of private cloud is that it offers increased agility to better meet changing business needs, both for user-based provisioning and for scaling resources in response to changing usage levels.

Determine which benefits are most important to your business, and use them to prioritize your goals and objectives. For example, the larger organizations we interviewed are confident that they can offer their own public cloud-like services cheaper, better, and more securely than external service providers. As a result, many are working to create a self-service, low-touch model that can be used to spin up new computing resources.

Other advantages that you might also consider in setting goals include the ability to:

- Offer cloud services that are designed specifically to meet your organization's unique business needs
- Decommission old assets such as operating systems, software, and hardware
- Create more cost-effective service offerings such as backup/recovery and disaster recovery
- Move entire data centers, simplifying and accelerating mergers and acquisitions

There are different cost, benefit, and service-level profiles for each computing environment. Set initial estimates of current state and desired future state for key measures in each environment.

Communicate your roadmap

We've already stated that a private cloud is built, run, consumed, and governed differently than a virtual consolidated infrastructure. The top performers we studied tell us that it's vital to communicate this difference. Follow their lead by creating a roadmap that lays out the path leading from the current state to the private cloud. Use the roadmap to communicate objectives, guide your efforts, and assess your progress.

Here's an example of a roadmap that takes you from a physical server environment to a predictive dynamic compute environment:

1. **Physical server environment**—The focus is on servers dedicated to specific applications. Capacity planning aligns server purchases with demand. Applications have high performance with dedicated resources.
2. **Permanent allocation of virtual servers**—The focus is on static consolidation of servers. Capacity planning and allocation of shared resources address peak usage. The results are higher utilization and lower unit cost.
3. **Proactive dynamic compute**—The focus moves to shared pools of computing resources. Capacity planning includes shifting resources to adjust to changing conditions. The result is highly flexible, cost-effective resource utilization.
4. **Predictive dynamic compute**—The focus becomes allocating shared resources in anticipation of demand. Capacity planning includes triggers based on historical usage patterns. The result is an even higher level of flexibility and more cost-effective resource utilization.

Establish baseline metrics

> *"Without the right metrics and processes in place, virtualization will get you into trouble faster. By first determining what measurements would have the most impact on the business, we are able to better assess what areas around people, process, and technology are best for our unique company requirements."*
> —JEFFREY D. TIBBITTS, CIO WINDSOR MARKETING GROUP

Adopting a portfolio view that encompasses physical, virtual, and private cloud resources can drive significant performance improvements. To demonstrate these improvements, you'll need effective measures in place. Here are some guidelines for establishing metrics that will help you track progress and communicate results:

- Where possible, segregate metrics by environment for more effective management of your computing environment portfolio.
- Normalize metrics to common units, such as sever level, some other logical unit of compute, or per application user, to facilitate comparison.
- Categorize costs and efforts as supporting either new initiatives or existing computing assets. Use measures that show how your private cloud strategy improves the efficiency of running existing assets, freeing resources for new initiatives.
- Present metrics in different ways to different stakeholders, such as IT management and staff, business funders of IT, application owners, and the executive team. Make sure you understand your audience well enough to know what data is meaningful to each segment.

Based on our work with top-performing organizations, we recommend measures in five areas to guide private cloud transformation efforts and quantify the service profiles of different computing environments: cost-efficiency metrics, agility metrics, service-quality metrics, operational metrics, and landscape metrics. Figure 4 summarizes some of the more frequently used measures.

Cost-efficiency metrics	*Description*	*Comments/considerations*
Capital cost	Annualized infrastructure cost, including maintenance for servers, network, and storage	Spreads purchase costs over useful life of asset
Resource utilization rate	Unit-level resource utilization, including server, network, memory, and storage as a proxy measure for capital cost efficiency	Shows differences in level of use of capital assets
Operating cost	Annual operational costs tied to unit level, including management costs (executive, audit, security), staff (development, operations, help desk), software (application, infrastructure), and facilities (power, cooling, space)	Breaks out other major ongoing unit-level cost drivers
Storage consumption	Annual cost of storage allocated to a particular unit; include base operating system (VMDK space) and shared space (application data)	Identify costs associated with additional storage requirements for each environment; consider tracking storage as a separate operating cost
Development and release efficiency	Calendar time and full-time-equivalent (FTE) hours to develop and deploy new workloads in each environment	Quantifies the effort for imaging, provisioning, testing, or production release for lifecycle efforts
Maintenance and support	Annual FTE hours and total cost of maintenance and support for existing workloads in each environment	Consider server-to-admin ratio or some other metric to normalize to the unit level
Agility metrics	*Description*	*Comments/considerations*
Service requests processed	Frequency and number of all service requests related to each computing environment	Overall activity may highlight opportunities to increase management efficiency
Self-service provisioning	Frequency of low-touch requests for new resources for each computing environment	Set goals and track progress to shift demand away from slower, higher-cost service request mechanisms
Release efficiency	The calendar and FTE time needed to deploy new workloads in different computing environments	Choose a measure that fits your business; consider the calendar and effort for release of all components of the service request, including efforts of various functional groups and time required for handoffs
Change success rate	Success rate of application and infrastructure changes in each environment	Consider measuring successful and failed rollbacks
Number of resource changes	Frequency of resource changes and workload movement in the private cloud	Higher frequency of resource changes should correlate with higher utilization rates
Aging	Duration of deployment of virtual environments for workloads in the private cloud	Consider tracking how many temporary workload deployments are extended beyond their initial decommission dates

Service-quality metrics	*Description*	*Comments/considerations*
Availability	Comparison of differences in availability or performance against SLAs for different computing environments	Measure the impact of the dynamic features that support higher availability
Planned maintenance	Average weekly planned maintenance hours	Determine the impact of different environments on the ability to complete maintenance during scheduled windows
Incidents handled by severity	Number and frequency of incidents by severity level for each environment	Determine the cost (resolution effort) associated with each incident type in each environment to refine unit-level operating cost values
Mean time to resolution	Time to resolve small, medium, and large outages in each environment	Determine variance of resolution rates by environment; if additional resource tiers are needed in the resolution process, determine if measures are still within agreed limits
Application performance	Overall reliability and performance of workloads as measured by application user experience	Compare for different environments and determine if there are measurable performance differences for different workload types
Customer satisfaction	How satisfied customers are with the services delivered from different computing environments	Determine if customer satisfaction is measurably different across environments
Operational metrics	*Description*	*Comments/considerations*
Certifications or training	Additional certifications or training required for the team to run new technologies	Develop short- and long-term plans for acquiring the necessary skills/people; determine the impact on operations; measure training effectiveness
Staffing	Administrator effort required for day-to-day operations	Examine how the number of administrators and workloads per administrator might increase or decrease
Resource effectiveness	Overall impact of new technology on quality of service	Determine if the technology creates unnecessary churn with users and/or lower-level support personnel; if current resources don't have the required skills, add experts to the team
Landscape metrics	*Description*	*Comments/considerations*
Physical	Number and percentage of total applications deployed in a traditional dedicated physical server environment	A small percentage of workloads may remain in physical environment due to specific performance issues
Virtual static	Number and percentage of total applications deployed in the virtual, consolidated environment	Static may include limited mobility, such as lift and shift during planned maintenance, failover, and DR
Private cloud	Number and percentage of total applications deployed in the private cloud environment	Work to increase the private cloud footprint to optimize both cost and agility
Consolidation ratio	Number of virtual machines per host in each environment	An indicator of workload density
Total slots, racks	The number and overall percentage of existing data center physical capacity used	

Figure 4. Balanced mix of metrics helps demonstrate the success of private cloud deployments.

With respect to cost-efficiency metrics, we strongly suggest adopting a unit-level costing scheme. Coarse-grained schemes that allocate costs at the business unit or enterprise level are generally not transparent or equitable. To have an apples-to-apples comparison of costs related to different computing environments or even external service providers, you must tie costs to such factors as annual cost per server, some other unit of compute, or to the application user. Annual unit costing also provides a powerful way to demonstrate cost reduction over time.

With respect to agility metrics, agility is particularly important for new workload deployments. Self-service access to pooled, virtualized resources can significantly reduce the time to provision new systems. Agility is also important for managing existing workloads. Efforts related to running what is already in place typically consume 60 to 80 percent of total IT budget.[14] Agility and the ability to respond quickly to changing conditions enable IT to manage higher workload density and higher levels of resource utilization.

Deploy proof of concept

> *"Not planning out the proper hardware, software, and infrastructure in the beginning can have a significant impact to your overall costs and cause unnecessary work. Be sure to plan to scale, and scale your plan based on the business projections for growth or economic factors that may impact that."*
>
> —MATT BAUSCH, SERVER ADMINISTRATOR, PEROT SYSTEMS

Remember that private cloud changes dramatically how IT is consumed, run, built, governed, and sourced. As a result, you need to address a wide range of changes as part of your larger-scale plans. We recommend you begin with a POC project to help you evaluate the people, process, and technology changes that will impact your organization.

Start with key objectives and competencies that you can adjust and refine as you progress through your POC. Here are some objectives you should include:

- **Gain executive buy-in.** Paradigm shifts do not occur without an executive champion. The IT champion for private cloud needs to actively realign the IT culture from a technology provider to a service provider. Also consider finding an executive champion from the user community. Identify a critical application that is a great fit for private cloud. Find its owner and you may have found your champion.
- **Establish a timeline, metrics, and roles/responsibilities.** Limit the POC duration to no more than six to eight months (two to three months for planning). Implement baseline metrics and establish the roles and responsibilities of each team member.
- **Secure dedicated resources.** Dedicate highly skilled resources with cross-functional experience to the POC team. Private cloud breaks down functional barriers. So tap your best people to help work out the policies, workflows, and automation needed for dynamic resource management.
- **Walk through the process before you automate.** Carefully walk through provisioning, resource adjustments, and *deprovisioning* using a set of representative workloads. You need to understand the workflow requirements, exceptions, and limitations before automating.

- **Review architecture and infrastructure.** Conduct a review of different infrastructure options. You may be able to use existing infrastructure resources. However, you should also consider unified computing platforms designed specifically for private cloud. These platforms, which integrate server, network, and storage resources, are now available from multiple vendors. Use the POC as an opportunity to evaluate new high-density server network clustering.
- **Identify technology.** Private clouds include more than just server virtualization. Identify all new technologies such as service catalog, service costing, metering, monitoring, and workflow tools you might need. Assess each as "must have" or "nice to have," or, alternatively, determine which need to be implemented immediately and which can be phased in after initial deployment.
- **Include legacy systems.** You need to identify and test legacy technology that you intend to integrate and include in workflow. Be sure to include systems management tools that do inventory, monitoring, and asset reporting. Try to avoid scope creep that comes from integrating everything during the POC.
- **Create requests for vendor participation.** Keep in mind that vendors may try to influence your requirements, and their recommendations may not match your company needs. It is best to identify your requirements first, create a request for information (RFI) list, and see how the vendors' solutions stack up to your needs. You may find that while some of the technology is cool, it may not meet your requirements.

Target workloads for private cloud

> *"Adopting a service portfolio view and matching applications to the right computing environment is critical for private cloud success. Creating the right application filter based on a few key attributes enables successful pairing of applications in private cloud environments."*
> —KALYAN KUMAR, WORLDWIDE HEAD OF CROSS FUNCTIONAL SERVICES, HCL TECHNOLOGIES LTD – ISD

Targeting workloads to the appropriate computing environment includes assessing the unique resource and performance attributes of the applications. Start by taking an inventory of applications and their attributes. If you have already broadly consolidated and virtualized servers, you may have done this inventory to a limited degree as part of your static virtualization targeting efforts.

As Figure 5 shows, targeting involves filtering applications at two levels:

- The first-stage filter determines the appropriate computing environment.
- The second-stage filter is used for workloads that are appropriate for private cloud. This filter helps identity the appropriate resource pool within the private cloud environment. There are multiple potential strategies for combining workloads on different hosts.
- You may need to revise filter criteria several times as your private cloud deployment evolves and as your level of automation increases. You can leverage these criteria to develop policies that guide automated resource-level changes and workload movement in Phase 4.

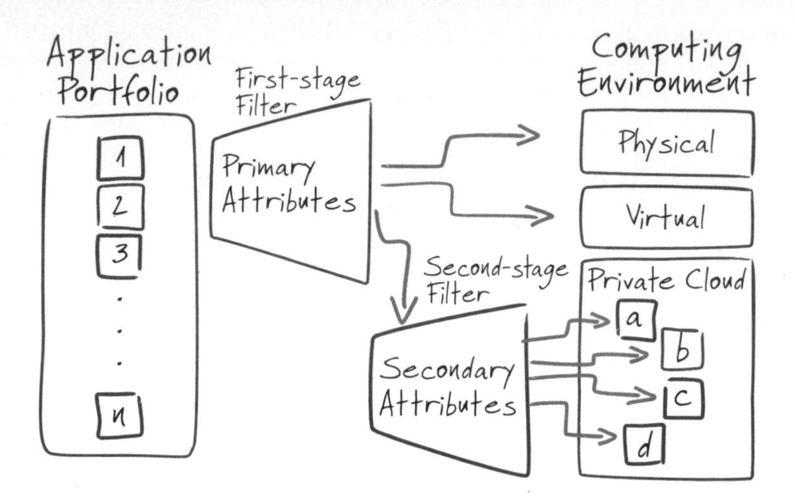

Figure 5. The first-level filter determines the appropriate computing environment for a workload; for private cloud workloads, the second-level filter determines the appropriate resource pool within the private cloud.

Consider a range of attributes to create primary and secondary filtering criteria, including:

- **Application classification**—Classify each application as mission critical (affecting customer), process critical (affecting internal process), or supporting (performing IT infrastructure monitoring and management). Don't reinvent the wheel. Leverage existing disaster recovery efforts to understand the business and IT classification scheme.
- **Workload type**—Determine if there are unique resource requirements, such as CPU, memory, I/O, network, physical cards, scanners, or point-of-sale devices, that might impact performance in a shared-resource environment.
- **Resource elasticity**—Use performance monitoring tools to determine if there are resource usage spikes. Calculate typical and peak performance differentials for CPU, memory, and storage, and determine if performance varies linearly based on the number of users.
- **Security and compliance**—Identify applications that are in scope for compliance or regulation. Determine if they need to be isolated to comply with regulatory, security, or business directives. Make sure proper approvals are in place internally and externally to test applications in a pilot scenario. Identify security requirements such as monitoring, virus protection, firewalls, and encryption.
- **Service levels**—Determine the SLAs for each application and determine what thresholds need to be monitored to ensure SLAs are met.
- **Connectivity**—Investigate network connectivity for the "last mile" and identify weak connections or hops between data centers that could impact outcomes. Look for opportunities to reduce the number of links or hops from servers to critical components such as databases.

- **Integration and dependency mapping**—Map virtual and physical relationships to facilitate troubleshooting, systems management, and asset inventory allocation. The map should show related systems required for proper function.
- **Management requirements**—Identify any unique tools required for patching, operating system updates, security, and backup that may be required for each workload in the virtual environment.

Initial efforts should focus on low-hanging fruit. It doesn't make sense to spend precious resources virtualizing workloads that are better left in the physical environment. Nor does it make sense to put workloads in a private cloud if they do not have usage spikes or if they do have strict compliance requirements.

Clean house

Now that you've set your goals, established baseline metrics, and targeted workloads to each computing environment, you're ready for the cloud, right? Wrong. You need to clean house first. The objective of this step is to remove unused workloads from physical and virtual environments before targeting applications for private cloud.

For each workload you assessed in the previous step, answer four critical questions: What do I have? Where is it? Who's using it? How much does it cost the business? You may discover hardware and applications that should be decommissioned because they are no longer in use. Decommissioning them avoids spending time and money virtualizing unused physical assets. It also allows you to get rid of unused virtual assets to free up resources for critical applications. One estimate is that up to 30 percent of virtual machines are zombies (virtual machines that haven't been used since initial deployment). As a rule of thumb, you should consider turning off assets that have not been used for two or more months.

The final housecleaning step is to redouble efforts around standardization before performing physical-to-virtual (P2V) migrations and before moving virtualized workloads to private cloud resource pools. Perform all P2V migrations on standard images wherever possible. Flag nonstandard configurations and replace them with golden builds now, or during subsequent upgrades and maintenance efforts.

Identify required competencies

> *"Conducting an initial discovery phase and identifying the key competencies checklists are essential for IT to maintain focus, execute, and report back measureable results. After all, vision without execution is merely hallucination."*
> —JOHN DODGE, SENIOR MANAGER, EUC PRACTICE, VMWARE

In this section, we present several people-, process-, and technology-related competencies that are vital to a successful private cloud initiative. We identified these competencies during interviews with top performers. Some of these competencies may evolve and others may emerge.

People competencies

> *IT workers may retain technical specialties, but they will need general skills that span the technology stack. CIOs should budget for cross-training programs and recruit skilled IT generalists in the future."*
> —MARK BOWKER, SENIOR ANALYST, ENTERPRISE STRATEGY GROUP, INC.

- **Tone at the top**—Executive sponsors should set the tone and promote two primary cultural changes. First, executives need to help shift the IT organization's mindset from a technology focus to a service provider focus. Second, executives need to highlight the increased need to follow process in a private cloud environment and help hold people accountable when they fail to do so.
- **Private cloud enterprise architect**—New role tasked with understanding the technical and business challenges, communicating them across functional silos, and creating a cohesive plan.
- **Service/product manager**—New role required to manage service lifecycle functions over time such as identifying customer needs, determining the core value proposition (cost, service quality, agility) of different resource environments, modeling costs, monitoring competitors' use of technology, and creating a service roadmap. Service/product managers can also gauge customer trends using customer satisfaction surveys.
- **Cross-domain expertise**—People with multiple domains of expertise and a systems view of infrastructure are required to deploy dynamic management of shared resource pools. People who understand key dependencies and touch points are critical for private cloud success.
- **Capacity management**—This is a critical skill in the private cloud because key resources may be allocated above 100 percent. Skilled capacity managers interpret historical performance and capacity data, compare it to current resource availability and usage patterns, and create dynamic, capacity-related policies and automated responses.
- **Resource policy management**—The development of policies and triggers that result in automated resource changes and workload moves is part art and part science. Getting the right mix of performance monitors and automation triggers is key to optimizing agility and resource utilization.
- **Automation**—What and how much should be automated is a complex question. To get the right answer, you need skilled people who have implemented automation and understand the tradeoffs between fixed and variable costs related to tooling, programming, and monitoring.
- **Administrators**—You need people who know how to manage virtualization in a dynamic environment and who understand the implications of moving from static to dynamic deployments. You'll need to train current server, network, and storage administrators; hire new people with the right skills; or engage the services of consultants or contractors.
- **Service desk**—Service desk agents need training to prepare them for applications and services in the private cloud. Cheat sheets and job aids with appropriate

escalation and other procedures ensure that agents know what actions to take. Assigning an engineer to serve as a subject matter expert for the service desk can be highly beneficial.

- **Application owners**—Application owners need to understand what changes to expect when their applications move to the cloud. Application developers should understand all hooks and monitoring requirements for the dynamic environment, and should establish backup and backout procedures to address emergencies.
- **Cross-functional teams**—Private cloud teams should include all key stakeholders, including security, audit, storage, networking, program management, application owners, and, if required, desktop engineering. The more technologies converge, the more functional groups will feel threatened if they are left out.

Process competencies

> *"It is a mistake when people think process inhibits innovation. It is quite the contrary. Process provides the ability for technologists to not have to worry about day to day and to focus on innovating."*
>
> —CINDY SCHUMACHER, VICE PRESIDENT OF GLOBAL INFRASTRUCTURE, EXPEDIA

- **Change management**—Current change definitions may impede your ability to dynamically lift and shift servers. As a result, administrators may be tempted to circumvent processes that aren't optimized for dynamic environments. To avoid this, leverage early virtualization experiences to help define, test, and refine new processes and change models.
- **Rollback**—Tested rollback plans enable you to recover quickly and minimize the impact on users and the business if you encounter problems with resource or workload changes.
- **Performance management**—Reports and measurements enable you to demonstrate adherence to SLAs. As you move to the cloud, you'll need to shift from resource-level performance to application- or workload-level performance. Remember, what business owners consider important often differs markedly from what IT people care about.
- **Root cause analysis**—Lack of tools, skills, and/or visibility of complex dependencies can hamper root cause analysis in the private cloud. To minimize this impact, revisit your support process. Assign a virtualization expert/engineer if necessary. Immediately escalate incidents related to private cloud resources until support strategies are documented. Initiate such approaches as reprovisioning from a snapshot versus determining point of failure to reduce resolution time and facilitate root cause analysis.
- **Asset inventory and reporting**—Ensure that the inventory system is virtualization aware. The dynamic nature of virtualization allows workloads to move from location to location (in many cases outside of standard change process). Consequently, the same asset might be counted multiple times against multiple systems. Test alternative ways of provisioning to avoid double counting.
- **Security and compliance**—Analyze security and audit processes for potential issues. For example, some top performers experienced issues of malware being bundled in

the virtual environment and unleashing a guest to host operating system attack. Specific measures around patching (not only virtual machines but also virtual operating system environments) must be in place and tested as part of the overall assessment. Appendix A and Appendix B provide more information on the impact of virtualization on audit and compliance.

- **Capacity management**—With virtualization, capacity management shifts from determining how many servers are needed to a more refined analysis of past usage and future requirements. Private cloud increases utilization in part by overallocating resources, which makes well-thought-out processes vital.

Technology competencies

> *"IT must first get an understanding of the needs of the business and second an understanding of the various architectures available for cloud computing—their pros and their cons—before starting to plan a large-scale rollout. Not all architectures or technologies will fit all solutions."*
>
> —CHARLTON BARRETO, TECHNOLOGY STRATEGIST AND PRINCIPAL ARCHITECT, INTEL

- **Virtualization**—Top performers have implemented broad use of virtualization at server, network, and storage layers. While many of them view private cloud as an extension of a broad virtualization deployment, others have pursued private cloud objectives at the same time as consolidation objectives.
- **Highly standardized infrastructure**—Standardized components should be identified at multiple layers of the computing stack. A loosely coupled strategy helps maintain flexibility while driving benefits of standardization. Version control, detailed dependency mapping, and associated ownership models are key to ongoing maintenance of standard images.
- **Overall automation**—Automation reduces manual tasks, such as processing of server patches, cloning of images, snapshotting and restoring backups, and ordering file and print servers. Automation also streamlines and speeds data tracking, workflow and approvals management, incident and problem management, and backup and recovery.
- **Automated provisioning**—A wide range of tools may be deployed to create a comprehensive solution that automates activities such as approval workflow, data collection, and run book. Don't forget that you must standardize these processes before you can achieve a high level of automation.
- **Automated resource scaling**—Tools and processes should be automated to coordinate resource changes and workload movement at the virtual level. Be sure to consider the complexity of a heterogeneous environment when planning automated workload moves.
- **Self-service catalog**—Self service requires some form of service catalog. Authentication by user or role and integration with a policy engine to determine the best deployment of service requests are also essential.
- **Policy engine**—Policies around the who, where, what, and when of new resource provisioning must be codified to support automation. Policies help in combining virtual servers on a common host. Later, you'll need to expand policies to determine

under what conditions resources are scaled up or down, as well as when workloads are moved to and from other resource pools.

- **Resource monitoring**—Monitoring collects the data that feeds the policy engine to trigger appropriate response. Tools must monitor process and resource performance, including physical and virtual CPU, memory, I/O, network, and storage. Additionally, the tools must monitor overall application performance from the user's perspective and provide this information to the policy engine.
- **Tool selection**—Management tools and processes must be able to handle both physical and virtual environments. To ensure flexibility, it's important to select tools and processes that support multiple virtual machine types and platforms.
- **Dependency mapping**—A virtualization and shared-resource environment has more resource dependencies than a dedicated physical environment. Application-to-asset mappings or basic application-to-application or asset-to-asset mappings ensure data accuracy in the dynamic and transient virtualized environment.
- **Activity-based costing**—Unique tools specifically designed to aggregate and report cost information may help service managers identify appropriate costs for primary service offerings, secondary services, and service level options.
- **Metering and chargeback**—There is no consensus on the use of chargeback. However, collecting data to accurately determine unit-level cost is important regardless of your internal billing mechanism. Data about resource usage also helps shape desired behavior in a resource rental model.

What you have accomplished in this phase

- Created a portfolio view of the infrastructure and established metrics and preliminary workload targets for three computing environments: physical, static virtual, and private cloud
- Set private cloud goals and objectives, and documented expected benefits for your private cloud initiative
- Developed a transformation model to communicate how your organization will evolve
- Implemented measures that capture cost, agility, service-quality, and operational and landscape performance
- Segmented measures by computing environment to highlight the different profiles of each
- Completed a private cloud POC that identified an infrastructure and architecture strategy, and secured necessary resources for successful rollout
- Inventoried applications along with their key attributes
- Targeted applications for each computing environment
- Decommissioned unused applications and removed zombie virtual machines
- Rebuilt nonstandard workloads using standard configurations where feasible
- Identified competencies for people, processes, and technologies that take into account the nature of dynamic, shared-resource management

Phase 2: Design services, not systems

"Achieving success in the cloud starts with the creation of an enterprise architect who is tasked with understanding the technical and business challenges, communicating them across functional silos, and creating a cohesive plan. The ideal design will incorporate not just technology but the blueprint for building new skills, processes, and technology required to deliver business-optimized services. Virtualization discussions need to be more than just a server consolidation discussion."
—DMITRY SHKLIAREVSKY, VICE PRESIDENT, PROFESSIONAL SERVICES, APPSENSE

What are you going to do?

In the previous phase, you refocused initial virtualization efforts to prepare for private cloud environments. You set objectives, established metrics, laid the groundwork for targeting workloads, eliminated clutter, and developed competency checklists to drive improvement.

Your goal in this phase is to meet the specific needs of the business by designing private cloud services. The focus is on enabling one-touch ordering of these services. Your mantra for this phase is, "Simplify the service offering to make sure the right things are built the right way."

Some organizations take a *consolidation project* approach to expanding the use of virtualization to increase ROI. However, a consolidation project driven by server footprint metrics is not business focused. Consolidation-focused efforts do not necessarily include process and infrastructure updates that are needed to optimize a virtual-heavy data center for responding to changing business needs.

Top performers have typically reached a point where they say, "Wait a minute, virtualization is a game changer. We need to rethink the IT services offered with this new technology." In fact, 58 percent of the companies we studied that are currently aggressively virtualizing production servers had at one point put adoption on hold and set out to improve operating procedures and shift their expansion strategy.[15]

Said another way, it isn't sufficient to replace physical servers with virtual servers. You must also update your service strategy.

It isn't sufficient to replace physical servers with virtual servers. You must also update your service strategy.

If you have made the shift from IT Infrastructure Library (ITIL®) V2 to ITIL V3, you may already have adopted a service-lifecycle approach to managing IT. A service-centric approach allows IT to offer custom services for the business that result in strong user demand for private cloud services. Demand drives increased adoption and that maximizes resource utilization.

Issues and indicators

In this phase, we address the following issues:

Issue	*Narrative Example:*
Consolidation efforts are focused on server count, not business needs.	"Our CFO wants to set consolidation targets. He calculates ROI based on how many servers have been virtualized and consolidated. Our strategy is to achieve 70 percent virtualization. We've done a lot of P2V conversions, but we can't scale enough skilled resources to support our goals. And our most highly skilled resources keep getting distracted with unique build requirements, which means that they also have to help production support with problem management and root cause analysis."
The IT staff has been force fed virtualization by the server admins and nobody understands how the new technology will help IT people do their jobs.	"Internal IT is resisting efforts to expand our virtualization footprint. The server admins have not explained the benefits of virtualization in terms that are meaningful to other IT groups. This is another example that reinforces our view that server admins are in their own little world. You can't relate to them. You can't talk to them. They don't care about anyone else's needs. I know there are tons of benefits to virtualization other than hardware savings. The admins just haven't explained it in way that helps us get on board with this effort."
Operating costs are eroding any savings we're getting from consolidation.	"Every build effort goes back and forth between our infrastructure team and the application developers. Our system specification process is weak. The business analysts tell us what they need. We build it. They say it's not what they need. We do it all over again. So there's a lot of wasted effort. What's worse, each server becomes a fragile artifact with a unique configuration."
We're seeing the same mistakes again and again.	"We've virtualized 20 percent of our production servers. That's 1,000 server conversions. We're focused on the target, but we don't document what we build, so we don't learn from our mistakes. Our team is really burned out. We have lost the will to go on. I'm pretty sure we will blow up before we finish the other 4,000 servers."
No, it's not "self server," it's "self service"!	"We've got a new portal where developers can request and get a new server provisioned in 15 minutes. But they want more than just a server. They want a development environment. We still use the old way to get network connectivity and storage. That means two days for the network and five days for storage, and the developers have to assemble the pieces. But, hey, who's counting?"
Do you want fries with that?	"I don't want a menu of 15 different tweaks that IT offers with my server. I want a fresh instance of a LAMP stack with the Perl script that my department has standardized on. Here's an idea, create a bundle for each of our five most requested services and put the bundles in the catalog."
Cut-tweak-paste systems are not documented.	"The cut-tweak-paste mentality of the server team has us using virtualization to generate a whole new batch of fragile artifacts. It's hard enough to support undocumented servers in a static environment. But now that they are in a private cloud pool, it's even worse. It's really starting to hurt production support. The only senior people who understand this stuff are thinking of leaving. I thought virtualization was going to make life easier."
Users ask for parts then hire consultants to put them together.	"The marketing folks sent a request for four virtual servers directly to the virtualization guy who was really behind. He hands back four servers and says, 'Here they are. Here's how you get into them.' Marketing went out and proceeded to install an entire web application across these four servers. Now we have customer data out in the clear where anybody can get at it. There's no specification around security. There's no specification around anything."
I'm from Missouri – the "show me" state.	"IT got this new cloud server option. We love the self-service provisioning. But putting critical apps in a high-density, shared resource space? They claim that with new and improved monitoring, they will automatically adjust resources or move the workload if performance falls. It sounds like a lot of things can go wrong. Can they deliver? I'll try the private cloud service for some low-priority apps first and see how it goes. If they do what they promised, then maybe I'll consider more business-critical workloads."

How are you going to do it?

The goal in this phase is to design business-optimized services and enable one-touch ordering. The actions that help achieve results include:

1. Adopt a service-design approach. Shift from framing virtualization expansion goals based on footprint and consolidation metrics to offering business-optimized services. Services that meet user needs will drive adoption. Widespread adoption is critical to driving cloud economics.
2. Simplify and standardize builds that include small, medium, and large configurations of infrastructure components. Servers are obvious, but don't forget to standardize network and storage resources as well.
3. Specify and certify templates that meet the specific needs of the environment (development, test, production); required performance and service levels; and security and compliance requirements (tooling, virus protection, and monitoring). Enable a golden build strategy that minimizes the number of different certified builds. Work to minimize variance in system configurations in the production environment.
4. Clarify deployment policies and service options. Service options include primary services, supporting services, and service level options. Policies determine who can deploy workloads, where and when they are deployed, and where and when supporting services are mandatory.
5. Leverage a service catalog to list primary services and service options. Codify policies to verify permissions, identify appropriate configuration templates, and target appropriate computing environments.
6. Adopt a bill-of-material (BOM) approach to building virtual resources. A BOM approach combines tiered standard server configurations, templates that include monitoring and management agents, and mandatory and optional services that can be ordered with each build.
7. Create a simple, repeatable, and predictable onramp to build and deploy resources. The focus is on applying engineering talent to refine the process used to release and retrieve servers and applications from production. The process must be tightly controlled—even more so than in the physical environment.

Design private cloud services

> *"An ounce of prevention is truly worth 20 pounds of cure when it comes to implementing a succinct private cloud strategy. Companies that take the time to discover real business problems and design business-optimized IT services are miles ahead of those that merely try to retrofit a service on top of what has already been implemented."*
>
> —JOHN DODGE, SENIOR MANAGER, EUC PRACTICE, VMWARE

If you build it, they will come. But only if you offer the right services, deliver them as promised, and reduce cost back to the business.

Deploying a private cloud requires a shift to a service orientation in IT. The widespread adoption of ITIL V3 is helping drive a shift in thinking from a siloed technology focus to a cross-functional, service-lifecycle focus. In a private cloud environment, the focus can't be limited to servers, switches, or storage devices. It must be expanded to include combinations of those components deployed to deliver services. Those services should be thoughtfully designed to meet specific business needs.

The top performers we interviewed strongly believe that it is just not possible to deploy a virtualized private cloud without a service-lifecycle approach. You can't offer self-service provisioning and manage shared resource pools and dynamic workloads if your organization and operational processes continue to operate as they did with the physical static infrastructure.

It's tempting to think that if you build a private cloud, users will come. They will, but only if you offer the right services, deliver them as promised, and drive value back to the business.

The service-design approach includes understanding user needs, defining services that meet those needs, and defining the functional and technical specifications needed to deliver those services. It also includes focus on optimizing the processes used to build and deploy virtualized workloads. These processes require clearly defined policies that specify what, how, where, and when virtual servers are deployed.

If you plan, specify, and certify per service specification using a repeatable set of building blocks, you can simplify a whole range of data center activities. Getting to the point where you can deploy new resources, adjust resource levels automatically, and deprovision resources when no longer used—all in a repeatable and highly automated fashion—requires having a service lifecycle methodology in place.

Why start with service design?

- **Maintain business alignment.** In a modern business, IT is almost always interposed between great ideas and business results. Private cloud is a great way for IT to accelerate the time from idea to results, but only if cloud services meet the needs of users. IT can design and launch service offerings and then evolve the offerings based on customer feedback, lessons learned, changing requirements, and maturity of technology.
- **Increase operational efficiency.** Although consolidation-related savings are increased by expanding the virtualization footprint, operational issues that result from inefficient build and run efforts can increase TCO. A service-driven approach that includes standardization and simplification minimizes build and run inefficiencies.
- **Optimize use of scarce resources.** Without a service-design approach that optimizes plan, build, and run efforts, the biggest bottleneck is often the highly skilled people needed to develop, deploy, and manage virtual resources.
- **Simplify automation.** A service-driven approach to virtualization helps standardize offerings, minimizing configuration and process exceptions that make automation problematic.

Organizations that pursue private cloud without service design may not realize that the process and controls built for a static siloed infrastructure don't fit the private cloud environment—until they experience issues. We recommend that you drive your private cloud rollout using a service-design effort as soon as the organization decides to deploy a private cloud strategy. In other words, if you are at or beyond the POC phase, shift gears now. When studying top performers, we've seen that somewhere between their initial virtualization deployments and their later use of virtualization to deploy private cloud resource pools for transient workloads, they have shifted to a service-design approach.

If you are at or beyond POC phase, shift gears to a service-design approach now!

There is a variety of service-design frameworks. For simplicity, we'll stick with a basic approach that defines four service elements:

- **Core service package**—Defines primary services and includes functional and technical specifications.
- **Supporting service**—Specifies functional and technical requirements for supporting services such as backup, HA/DR, support priority, maintenance windows, security, and firewall or network configurations.
- **Service level option**—Defines available service levels and priorities, addressing such factors as performance, resource allocation (CPU, memory, IO, network, storage), business impact, recovery, and MTTR.
- **Cost**—Lists the annual unit cost for each service. Service cost estimates will be refined in Phase 4. However initial estimates should be used when designing services.

We recommend the following activities when defining private cloud service packages:

- **Understand business needs.** Begin by gaining an understanding of what the business needs are. Do existing IT services meet those needs? What are the factors that impact demand? Cost? Service level? Flexibility? Work with business process and application owners to understand how current services can be improved.
- **Categorize users.** Are there common types or classes of service requestors? Do they have needs that are common by type? Do they have different purchase authorities or different read/write permissions? Are there processes and workflows defined to verify approval and grant service requests?
- **Inventory existing services.** Are current services defined and clearly presented to service requestors and consumers? Are methods for requesting IT services published and followed?
- **Categorize workloads.** Revisit the workload classification you used in Phase 1 to target each computing environment. Look for obvious groupings based on attribute data. Let the data define certain types of service offerings—for example, the number of web app servers with large CPU and memory requirements or the number of database servers with few connections and significant ROM requirements.

- **Categorize platforms.** What are the computing platforms and operating systems that support the workloads targeted for the private cloud? What are standard platform and stack requirements? What are the development environments, databases, web servers, and middleware? What standard software applications are used in the environment—for example, SharePoint, Drupal, or Project? What are the essential, desirable, and optional management tools and agents?
- **Understand current usage patterns.** Are there predictable usage trends for different workloads? For example, end-of-month financial applications may require more resources for certain periods during each month. Other applications may have heavy usage during business hours.
- **Consider service level and performance requirements.** What are the uptime requirements? Planned maintenance windows? Service support SLAs? Backup requirements? High availability and disaster recovery failover requirements? Multisite redundancies?
- **Categorize security and compliance requirements.** Do workloads include sensitive data? Are workloads to be accessed via the internal network or from the external network by customers, partners, and suppliers? Are workloads subject to regulatory compliance? Keep in mind that security risks are amplified by automation.

After initial assessment of these areas, common patterns should emerge. Look for obvious service offerings. Consider bundles of services that are frequently combined for specific users. Develop a matrix of service packages and supporting service offerings and identify specific combinations that are mandatory and optional at different service levels.

Specify resource templates

> *"Standardizing on small, medium, and large server configurations while specifying and certifying templates for different environmental, performance, security, and compliance requirements is HUGE. I don't think it can be overemphasized how hard this is to do in the physical world, and how easy in virtual."*
>
> —SCOTT VAN DEN ELZEN, SENIOR SYSTEMS ARCHITECT, IP SERVICES

Virtualization allows administrators to cut, tweak, and paste server images, which can increase the number of fragile artifacts in the infrastructure. Without rigorous standardization of server templates, every tweaked image results in yet another nonstandard server in production, driving up costs, errors, effort, and frustration.

If each server is different you can't standardize services, you can't automate, you can't guarantee results, you can't reduce touches, and you can't free up resources. If, on the other hand, servers are highly standardized, then even exceptions can achieve a high degree of reliability.

The goal here is to create a set of standard server configurations and templates that meet the requirements of most workloads. Having most of your virtual servers use standard-build images reduces administration effort and eliminates the tendency to create fragile artifacts. Standard configurations in production simplify and speed deployment, improve troubleshooting, and increase the efficiency of global changes.

If you focus your highly skilled resources on building a process to specify and certify templates, you can reduce the amount of resource-burning back-and-forth effort between application development and infrastructure teams (*build thrash*). Standard builds also reduce the skill requirements for build and support functions, and they reduce the amount of time required by new employees to learn server configurations.

We recommend using the following steps to create a set of standard server configurations and templates:

- Start by creating a process to specify and certify server templates. Include procedures for creation, storage, access, and update. Include a version control mechanism. However, don't go overboard with process design. Start with the basics and refine processes as you use them over time. Putting effort into refining processes will pay dividends in the form of reduced build thrash, better production efficiency, and higher service levels.
- Specify a set of small, medium, large, and extra-large resource configurations. Work from an inventory of the workload types currently in use. Identify a mix that meets 80 percent of current use cases. If you already have standard server configurations, convert and refresh them for virtualization.
- Identify templates for different infrastructures, platforms, and software services, and for different workload types such as file/print, web, database, and financial.
- Identify templates for development, test, and production. These different environments may require different monitoring applications, administrative agents, or backup tools.
- Identify requirements for multiple data centers if you have them. You might want to consider cloning a single template to each data center and then making any needed modifications to that clone, such as for network time protocol (NTP) servers, for each data center.

A general approach is to create a set of base templates. The base templates include mandatory components such as anti-virus. You can then copy and modify the base set to create a second set that includes management agents. Next you can copy and modify the second set to create a third set that includes other optional services such as backup agents. For additional unique services, you can install the required software upon the final deployment of the appropriate templates.

Overall, separate components (servers, operating system, applications, middleware, and database) and settings (data, personality, and options) as much as possible. Virtualization is about abstraction, which requires resources to be flexible. So they must be loosely rather than tightly coupled. Think federation, not integration.

Keeping a template current typically involves converting the template to a virtual machine, updating anti-virus signatures, operating system patches, and other tool upgrades, and then converting the virtual machine back to a template. Be sure to identify tools for detecting and tracking drift on all baseline templates.

Clarify build and deployment policies

> *"In complex application architectures, the tendency can be to create dev/test/training environments that are scaled-down versions of production environments. As your initial virtualization efforts begin to bear fruit, take advantage of the technology's strengths in provisioning to create those additional supporting environments with retention and replication of all the moving parts and relationships found in production."*
> —LOUIS TROISE, CONSULTANT

To get to the point where services are listed in a service catalog and service deployment actions are automated, you need build and deployment policies that can be codified. So if your policies are not clearly documented, you should clean them up and document them now, even if you aren't at the point where you dynamically allocate resources based on service requests. Policies need time to age and adjust to the particulars of your environment. They will likely shift over time. If you move to automated deployment before policies age, you may end up trying to automate a moving target.

As Figure 6 shows, you need two types of policies: build policies and deployment policies. Your build policies should guide the selection of the appropriate template for virtual servers deployed. They should also define the supporting service offerings appropriate for the deployment environment, such as monitoring and management tools, run book automation workflows, HA/DR, backend system integrations, approval workflows, and reporting and backup agents. Moreover, they should define the service priorities to be assigned.

Once you have created build policies that guide the build package, you need to create deployment policies that define deployment criteria. Is the workload a good fit for the private cloud environment? If so, is there a specific host or resource pool that should receive the workload?

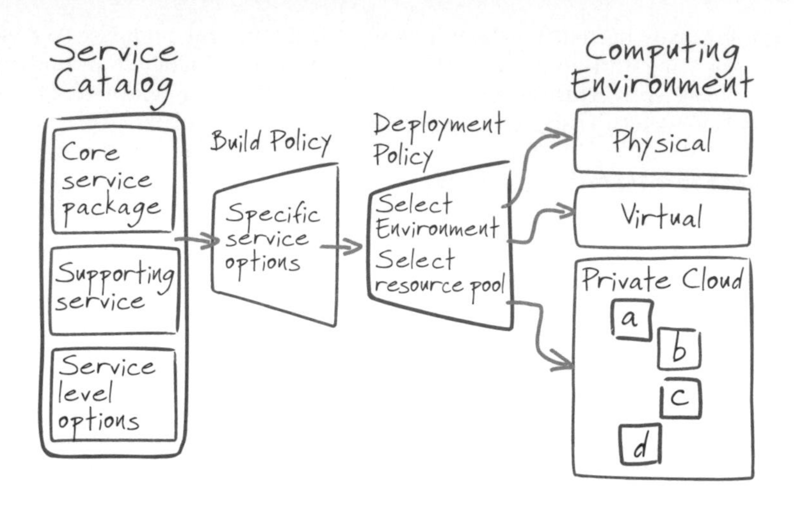

Figure 6. To get to the point where services are listed in a service catalog and service deployment actions are automated, you need to codify build and deployment policies.

To deploy services according to policy, you need information that provides context for the service request. Part of the service request process should therefore include asking questions that help you gain the information needed to satisfy the policy.

- Who is requesting the service? Is the requestor authorized to make that request? Ideally, you should reveal only those service options that are appropriate to the requestor.
- What will the requested resource be used for? Development? Production? Will it include sensitive information? The template used to deploy the requested resources depends on the type of workload.
- Where will the service be deployed? A template for a web application deployed outside the firewall should have different components than one used for an application deployed inside a secure perimeter.
- How long are the resources needed? A transient workload may be deployed on a different host than a workload with a long life.

Are your security and compliance policies established and documented? If not, you should consider doing it now. It's one thing to consolidate existing servers through P2V. It's another thing altogether to receive a request for a new server and automatically deploy it in a way that meets security and compliance requirements.

Service list or catalog

It's great to be able to use a self-service portal to request and get a new server provisioned in 15 minutes. But it's not so great if you have to wait two days for network connectivity. What users want is a mechanism for entering one-touch orders. A one-touch order gives users the opportunity to select a bundle or build a service request from list of service offerings, supporting services, and service levels.

The physical manifestation of your service offering and policies is the service request form. The service list on the form should be actionable and usable to initiate service requests and automatic deployment. Service request processing should be tied, through workflow, to authorization and service fulfillment processes. The information solicited from the requestor on the service request form should be sufficient to drive the resulting build work order.

It's great to get a new server provisioned in 15 minutes. But it's not so great if you have to wait two days for network connectivity.

A comprehensive service request and fulfillment mechanism includes:

- **Primary services list**—The list of services should be actionable, more than merely a menu of services. It should provide the ability to order and track services. If it's only a menu, then the service request would have to be submitted elsewhere for processing. That would add a step, which may discourage adoption.
- **Supporting services list**—The mechanism should show mandatory and optional supporting services based on the requestor's answers to attribute questions. It should also show the cost of supporting services.
- **Service-level options**—The mechanism should indicate service-level options and associated costs (think gold, silver, and bronze SLAs). Production servers with certain SLAs may require templates that include monitoring and backup, HA, and DR agents. The highest level SLAs may require failover or even redundant data centers.
- **Role-based entitlement**—Users should be allowed to view only those services that they are authorized to procure or check out. Tie the service list to user credentials and hide service options not available to the requestor.
- **Security and compliance policies**—Provide clearly defined indication of services that can and cannot be requested based on planned usage. For example, clearly state that business owners or application developers of regulated applications cannot apply for resources located on public domains without C-level approval.
- **Integrated service offerings**—Bundle services into packages that make sense to requestors. For example, a "Developer LAMP stack," "Marketing Website," or "Collaboration Toolset" package should include everything needed for the most common use cases. It's important to include integrated provisioning in the packages to ensure timely delivery of the service.
- **Deployment duration**—Allow specification of how long a compute resource is required. Let users enter the beginning and end date. Provide guidelines for fixed, variable, and event-driven end dates and specify what happens when the end date is reached. For example, will the resource be deprovisioned immediately or is there a grace period? Notify the user when the end date is approaching.
- **Automatic end of lifecycle**—The mechanism should automatically deprovision resources and return them to resource pools when certain defined thresholds are met. End-of-life activities should include such items as usage reporting, showback/chargeback, and license harvesting.

- **Backup and recovery**—The mechanism should store decommissioned virtual machines and related data for a specified period of time, permitting recovery of those that have been inadvertently decommissioned.
- **Chargeback and/or showback**—You may choose not to implement formal chargeback with your private cloud. However, identifying the cost for each service helps shape user behavior toward a service rental model. Cost can be listed as "information only" (showback). If you do move toward chargeback or showback, determine if it will be based on resource allocation, usage, or other factors. Clearly indicate the costs associated with different service options.
- **Approval workflow**—Use workflows for fully or semi-automated approval of service requests. Include transparency and automated communication to indicate request status. Show major steps in the build process. Status updates help users gain an understanding of what IT does and helps build trust, which is key for driving the demand for virtual services.
- **Use terms appropriate to users**—Don't use an "inside-out" list of IT terms. Use service design efforts to understand what users need. Present service offerings in terms they understand.
- **Encourage a virtualization first policy**—Indicate the cost differential for virtual versus physical. Make it clear that physical server requests require justification and exception approval. Get help from executive sponsors to enforce the policy and discourage users from going around IT to third-party providers.

An effective service request mechanism is a key building block for moving toward a resource rental model. Ironing out a semi- or fully automated process for service provisioning is a great way to build competencies for full automation needed later to adjust workloads in response to usage spikes.

A repeatable approach to build and deploy

> *Automating a mess yields an automated mess. You need standardization, governance, and processes. Furthermore, getting proven operational controls right with the virtualized foundation is an absolutely necessary first step to evolving it to a successfully implemented private cloud."*
> —GORDON HAFF, CLOUD EVANGELIST, RED HAT

In this phase, you have defined core services, supporting services, and service levels. You have specified and certified templates that meet a variety of requirements including security and compliance. Now the goal is to create the process to build and release virtual workloads with consistent and predictable results.

The ease of deployment of virtual servers amplifies both the power and the risk of virtualization. Virtualization makes it so easy to copy and paste that admins in many IT shops are hacking more than building. They take a server already built, customize it, and then push it out. They take specified templates that are a 60 percent fit and customize them. They create fragile artifacts with each release. That's a recipe for disaster in the highly automated private cloud environment.

Even with the power of templates, some of the low-performing IT organizations we studied experience resource bottlenecks with deployment. One organization we interviewed has four or five highly qualified engineers who were continually experiencing significant build thrash whenever developers requested a development environment. The developers would order an environment and the virtualization admins would build it. When the build didn't work the way the developers expected, they'd throw it back to the admins. This build thrash required the highly skilled and resource constrained admins to redo the work multiple times just to get the environment to work.

Top performers invest in production engineering skills to document what happens at each step, and they fine tune the process to drive out sources of variation.

The *thrash* was occurring because there was no build process to provide an accurate level of specification upfront. What's more, the engineers didn't document the steps they took to modify the original build template. They were wasting time and building fragile artifacts with every effort. When it came time to support the new server and do root cause analysis, the only thing they could recover or trace out of the process was the original email message with requirements that didn't work.

Top performers, on the other hand, put significant effort into the preproduction build process. They assign their best people to process development and architecture design. They manufacture each server using a service list and standard configuration approach, and use checklists or workflow engines to ensure that process is consistently followed. They recognize that manufacturing to meet service definitions typically requires resources and effort from multiple groups and teams. Only in that way can they successfully build and deploy the requested services. These top performers invest in production engineering skills to document what happens at each step, and they fine tune the process to drive out sources of variation.

To effectively manage resources in a private cloud environment, you need to create a path to build a server that is repeatable and dead-on, and has almost no variance. The combination of specified and certified configurations and templates, along with a list of required and optional supporting services, makes this possible. Success depends on having well-defined and optimized build and release process and backend tools that produce the right builds every time.

Release engineers specify and certify the build components. The operations staff typically uses the build process to provision production.

In creating the process, consider the following:

- **Integrated build**—Combine standard configurations, templates, and other services into a single build. A quality assurance team may test and certify the build in a preproduction environment to verify that it is stable and functional.
- **Workflow**—The build and deploy process can be debugged using a checklist to make sure the steps are followed in order every time. However, some type of workflow engine or run book automation tool is needed to execute tasks in order to provision a one-touch service order.
- **Process**—Keep in mind that manufacturing a production-worthy service typically involves multiple people and departments as well as multiple system components.
- **Verify service**—Production service verification ensures that the system is working and stable in the production environment. Monitoring tools should be activated and baselines set for performance and availability.
- **Tracking**—Be sure to track the release of new systems into production. Record workflow and signoff steps. Create server IDs. Record all data to facilitate support and leave an audit trail.

The build and deploy processes are best managed with some type of workflow tool. This removes the need for personnel to verify approvals. It also leverages automation to reduce the number of manual tasks. Workflow tools can be triggered by virtualization tool events in a semi-automated workflow. Workflow tools can also handle tracking and recording activities.

You have to have a repeatable, proven process before you can automate it. Otherwise automation simply accelerates bad process and you end up moving backwards ever faster. Automation should be applied to the build and release workflow as much as is feasible. It's important to note, however, that manual or semi-automated workflow combined with process improvement helps refine process so you end up with something worth fully automating.

Make build knowledge public

Many IT organizations rely on tribal knowledge. Even in large shops, informal communication and hoarding knowledge is common. While relying on email, text messages, and phone conversations may preserve the value of technical expertise in a siloed organization, it kills progress in a cross-functional cloud environment. It keeps IT organizations stuck at a level of maturity in which they never capture lessons learned.

Without publicly documenting process, specification, and certification, it is difficult to feed back improvements that keep the same mistakes from recurring.

IT organizations that keep critical knowledge private waste effort during both build and support efforts. Many organizations that don't document process and build efforts soon become resource constrained and end up building and deploying systems in a hurry.

IT staff members in a large IT shop were convinced they didn't have enough skilled resources to build virtual systems at the required rate, so they brought in virtualization contractors to ease backlog. They found, however, that nothing had been documented, making it difficult to bring new staff up to speed. Consequently, the highly skilled staff and contractors were still bogged down in the job of building virtual systems. The key lesson learned was that the highly skilled engineers should be focused on specifying and certifying builds and fine tuning process to simplify work and better leverage lower-skilled staff.

This shop was hit with a double "lack of documentation" whammy in that the skilled resources were also repeatedly pulled into production support efforts. That's because the engineers didn't document what steps they took to modify the original build templates. So there was almost no documentation to guide support staff when it came time for root cause analysis.

To prevent these types of issues, the objective in this step is make critical knowledge public in order to learn from mistakes and simplify build and production support. Achieving this objective involves four activities:

1. Documenting the build process and practice process improvement to stop repeating resource-consuming mistakes
2. Documenting builds to optimize root cause analysis and facilitate service support
3. Ensuring that documentation is updated and version controlled
4. Standardizing requirements for training to avoid deviation from established procedures and processes created for new technologies and services

Top-performing organizations rely heavily on process and build documentation to leverage skilled work and make everyday work easier. An IT executive from one highly efficient organization was adamant that focus on process and knowledge management was a critical success factor in the organization's broad use of virtualization. He said that all their process work and knowledge management paid off when they were able to integrate a recent merger in only three months. It is much easier to integrate systems and bring new staff up to speed when process steps and work activities are clearly spelled out.

Here are some considerations for making critical knowledge public:

- Start with an acknowledgement that virtualization can create problems in that it abstracts and obscures. Virtualization requires cross-functional generalists who understand how everything works together, and there is a scarcity of that type of skill. It's important, therefore, to assign these generalists to process and documentation so they can offload more focused work to specialists.

- Get process religion. Process ensures effective build and deploy efforts. Consider hiring process engineers to help document and improve virtualization-related processes. The cost of this upfront work will more than pay for itself over time through lower TCO.
- Be sure to implement a process that makes it easy to create documentation and keep it up to date.
- Capture lessons learned so you don't repeat mistakes. Measure instances of repeat mistakes and focus the organization on eliminating thrash.
- Make everyday work easier. Virtualization drives impressive consolidation-related savings. It makes cut and paste of servers possible. But keep in mind that TCO is driven by how many times the staff has to touch servers. Leverage process and knowledge management to eliminate dependence on tribal knowledge and make everyday tasks easier.

What you have accomplished in this phase

- Created functional and technical specifications and preliminary cost estimates for core service packages, supporting service offerings, and service-level options
- Defined a set of standard system configurations (server, network, storage)
- Created standard resource templates that meet the requirements of most workloads
- Defined templates for different platforms, for variations related to test, development, and production environments, and for different data center locations
- Deployed a service catalog that lists core service packages, supporting services, service levels, and costs for each item
- Established build and deployment policies
- Established a repeatable build process that generates builds to meet service requests, automates workflow, verifies service, and tracks activities
- Created a process to capture build-related knowledge to facilitate maintenance and support

Phase 3: Orchestrate and optimize resources

"Private cloud computing is a paradigm shift that requires not only understanding new technologies but also how they impact current systems and processes around your overall service delivery and design. Having a very clearly defined workflow that points back to measurable impact on overall return on equity for the business is imperative to determining if the new architecture is working."
—RICH MCGINTY, DIRECTOR OF IT, METLIFE

What are you going to do?

In the previous phase, you specified and certified private cloud services. You enabled one-touch ordering. You also optimized build activities to ensure that the resources released into the private cloud are predictable and reliable.

In this phase, the goal is to optimize private cloud service delivery by increasing automation. We will update infrastructure as well as monitoring and tooling to enable low-touch management of dynamic workloads. Your mantra in this phase is, "Automate response to optimize service levels."

This is a critical phase for building business confidence. The notion introduced in Phase 2 that, "If you build it they will come," only works if you build the right thing, if it works as promised, and if it delivers greater business value.

This is the phase in which you prove that private cloud services work as promised. If you don't deliver cloud services to meet the service requirements of the business, users might lose confidence and go to third-party service providers, thereby jeopardizing overall success of your private cloud initiative.

This is the phase in which you prove that private cloud services work as promised.

Automation is key to deploying and managing private cloud resources. From a user perspective, automation enables the on-demand capabilities of private cloud that drive business agility. These include one-touch ordering of new services and real-time scaling of resources to respond to changing usage levels. From an internal IT perspective, automation enables the capabilities that drive down the unit cost of private cloud services, thereby increasing value. These capabilities include low-touch orchestration and rightsizing of infrastructure to optimize resource utilization.

Automation efforts in a private cloud environment should be focused on responding to self-service requests, monitoring and responding to changing workload conditions, and deprovisioning resources that are no longer needed. Additional opportunities for automation include eliminating repetitive and error-prone activities that consume so much senior staff time.

Retooling infrastructure to handle movement of large workloads is critical. Rationalizing, consolidating, and integrating monitoring and tooling to identify and respond to changing usage levels is also key to maintaining application performance. In this phase, you will update service management processes to include higher levels of automation, and you will document automation, tooling, and workflow to minimize production resource inefficiencies.

Issues and indicators

In this phase, we address the following issues:

Issue	*Narrative Example:*
We have way too many exceptions in production.	"We congratulated ourselves on finally ensuring that most of our production servers are standard builds. But virtualization has given server admins a cut-tweak-paste power that has spawned a whole new batch of snowflakes. Now we struggle to support, patch, and upgrade these fragile artifacts in the private cloud environment. Can't we automate this tweak-prone processes to cut out the temptation and means for mischief?"
Our backlog of critical projects is getting bigger and bigger.	"Senior staff needs to get more aggressive with tier-1 and mission-critical applications, not to mention other important projects that are taking a back seat during consolidation efforts. We're desperate to free up time for these highly skilled guys so they can focus on projects that will make the business more successful. Instead, they're spending their time on day-to-day implementation and troubleshooting."
It seems like we just keep making the same mistakes again and again.	"The server guys aren't documenting how to upgrade and maintain standard systems, let alone the fragile artifacts they create. Production support doesn't have the skills to do root cause analysis. It feels like we are always calling in the cloud architects for support. And because they aren't documenting lessons learned, we can't manage similar issues in the future without involving them again. It feels like a death spiral. I thought private cloud was all about efficiency. What happened?"
It's becoming clear that the architecture doesn't support our private cloud strategy.	"The CIO keeps asking us to do more with less. I get that. That's reality in the IT world. But who set the expectation that we could drastically expand our virtualization footprint, set up a shared-resource environment, and manage mobile workloads using the same infrastructure, licenses, staffing, and budgets? To do this right, we need to upgrade servers, networks, storage, and other components. I understand the economics of utilization. But we have to spend money now to save money later. If we had known this when we set our private cloud targets, we could have built the appropriate budget and procured the right hardware to begin with."
Insufficient capacity is driving down performance.	"The architect decided to use existing servers for our private cloud. Then we discovered they weren't able to host multiple virtual machines without taking a performance hit. Now, performance numbers in the shared-resource environment are terrible and we've had a 15-month delay because of that decision."
Our monitoring and tooling just don't cut it in a dynamic environment.	"We're facing up to the fact that our current tooling isn't up to the job of managing mobile workloads in a shared-resource environment. Our tools lack the monitoring and controls we need to manage this dynamic infrastructure."
Performance and capacity management is more art than science.	"Our performance and capacity management efforts have been very tech focused. Now we have service definitions and commitments. We need to monitor performance at an aggregate level. That performance data feeds capacity decisions. Sure, fine-tuned utilization helps our numbers. How much resource should we allocate to a workload? When do we respond to changing performance variables? How much do we increase workload density? Who has time to figure out the nuances of how to automate these decisions?"

How are you going to do it?

The goal is to optimize private cloud service delivery by automating low-touch response to changing resource usage levels. The actions that help achieve results include:

1. Ratchet up the level of automation, to enable key processes central to the private cloud value proposition. This includes provisioning workloads in response to self-service requests; responding to conditions that require resource adjustment and movement of mobile workloads; and deprovisioning resources that are not in use.
2. Retool the infrastructure to deploy private cloud shared resources by updating servers, network, storage, and other components as needed.
3. Improve monitoring to detect when resource changes or workload moves are required. Increase focus on user-facing application performance. Consolidate toolsets where feasible to create a single pane of glass for managing physical and virtual resources.
4. Optimize service management processes to manage dynamic workloads and meet private cloud SLAs.
5. Develop and document a run book to reduce the need for experts to handle maintenance and service support. Focus on continual process improvement, capturing lessons learned and shifting routine work away from the most highly skilled staff.

Expand automation

> *"Automation should be approached with caution by starting with simple tasks first. Learn from early projects and measure results before proceeding."*
> —MARK BOWKER, SENIOR ANALYST, ENTERPRISE STRATEGY GROUP, INC.

Fulfilling the promise of private cloud requires higher levels of automation than are possible in virtual static or physical environments. Although automation can play a key role in improving efficiency and shifting work away from highly skilled administrators in any environment, its purpose in private cloud is more far reaching:

- Automation enables one-touch provisioning. Real-time response to service requests includes a range of activities than can be coordinated and automated via a workflow solution.
- Automation enables rightsizing of resources. Real-time performance monitoring and response includes adding and removing resources available to a particular workload.
- Automation enables lift and shift. Real-time performance monitoring and response may also include moving virtualized workloads to and from different resource pools.

Rightsizing resources and lifting and shifting workloads after periods of heavy usage are key to an IaaS strategy.

The goal in this phase is not to implement end-to-end automation. Rather, it is to begin putting pieces in place to streamline response to different private cloud actions. Take known good sets of related tasks and automate them. You can achieve quick wins through partial automation incorporating both automated and manual procedures. Leverage both run book automation and vendor-supplied tools that manage different physical and virtual resources. These tools can automate the overall run book, not only across virtual but also across physical stacks.

You will automate three key processes to optimize private cloud service delivery.

One-touch provisioning

The first process you will automate is the provisioning of workloads. Full automation of one-touch provisioning in this phase builds on the pieces put in place for one-touch order in Phase 2. In Phase 2, you defined services, standardized configurations and templates, clarified build and deployment policies, and developed a repeatable process for build and deploy. If you are using a service catalog or request portal for one-touch ordering, then automated one-touch provisioning integrates a series of steps that fulfill user-initiated service requests.[16]

Things to consider for one-touch provisioning:

- Never say no to somebody who wants to provision resources (assuming they have authorization to request services). They need to know that resources are always available and are provisioned consistently and predictably.
- Use attribute data collected by the service catalog to feed the build and deployment policy engine. Policies should determine who has authority to request resources, and, based on planned usage, which computing environment is appropriate for the request. (Not all requests will be provisioned in the private cloud area.)
- Use a workflow engine to verify that resources are available and functioning, execute build and deployment steps, and then verify that provisioning has been successful. Failed verification should trigger automated rollback and exception notification and response process.
- Include software license tracking and chargeback reporting to ensure accounting of all components deployed in the build.
- Include automated notification to both requestors and system administrators.
- Use hooks to collect data that can direct various workflow steps. As you move from partial to full automation, maintain a record of steps taken in log files that allow administrators to see that automation is working.
- Use workflow to collect data from the various tools involved and update the configuration management system (CMS) or other asset registry with all pertinent information.

Resource changes and workload moves

> *"Once the provisioning of standardized services is automated, a discipline of continuous improvement is necessary—rapid, cross-functional sensing and responding to daily changes in the environment. The ideal mix of standardization, agility, and quality can thus be achieved and sustained."*
>
> —STEVE BELL, CO-AUTHOR OF *LEAN IT: ENABLING AND SUSTAINING YOUR LEAN TRANSFORMATION*

The second process you will automate is the orchestration of resources. This includes changing resource allocation within a resource pool, and moving workloads between resource pools. Low-touch orchestration of resources enable higher resource utilization and workload density.

Utilization levels in private cloud environment should exceed those of advanced static virtualization deployments which range from 20 to 40 percent for basic virtualization, and 40 to 60 percent for advanced consolidation. Top-performers we studied have targeted greater than 60 percent utilization for their private cloud deployments.[17]

Workload density can also be optimized by an automated resource orchestration. Organizations tend to increase workload density, as measured by the consolidation ratio (number of virtual machines per host), as they gain experience with capacity and resource management. However, depending on the type of workload, resource orchestration can enable workload densities of 11 to 25 or more virtual machines per host.[18]

We'll go into more detail about strategies for optimizing resource adjustments and workload moves in Phase 4.

For now, focus on optimizing the workflow. You should codify resource policy based on service level requirements and business priorities of different workloads. Monitoring tools may provide input to the policy engine to trigger automated response based on predefined conditions. As you re-architect your infrastructure in this phase, it's essential to create initial resource pool deployments to enable resource optimization and workload mobility.

Things to consider for automated resource adjustments:

- **Integrate resource policy with workflow.** Your policies should determine under what conditions resources are changed or workloads are moved.
- **Include security and compliance requirements.** Security and compliance controls may limit the types of automated response. For example, moving a workload to a host with a different OS patch level may not be allowed.
- **Use business priority.** The risk profile of workloads should be considered when making change versus move decisions.
- **Watch out for performance issues caused by frequent workload moves.** Investigate cause and modify workflow rules to eliminate degradation.

What is the payoff? Perhaps the most important payoff in the user's mind is the automatic upward adjustment in resources to ensure high service quality in the event of rising usage levels. Managing your private cloud infrastructure at high workload density may reduce capacity available for usage spikes. Automating resource adjustments means the user never knows that their workload was running out of resource.

The payoff for IT and the business is the cost efficiency resulting from the automatic downward adjustment in resources as usage levels fall. It's this reallocation of resources back to overhead or to other workloads that optimizes resource utilization. Figure 7 illustrates this dual payoff.

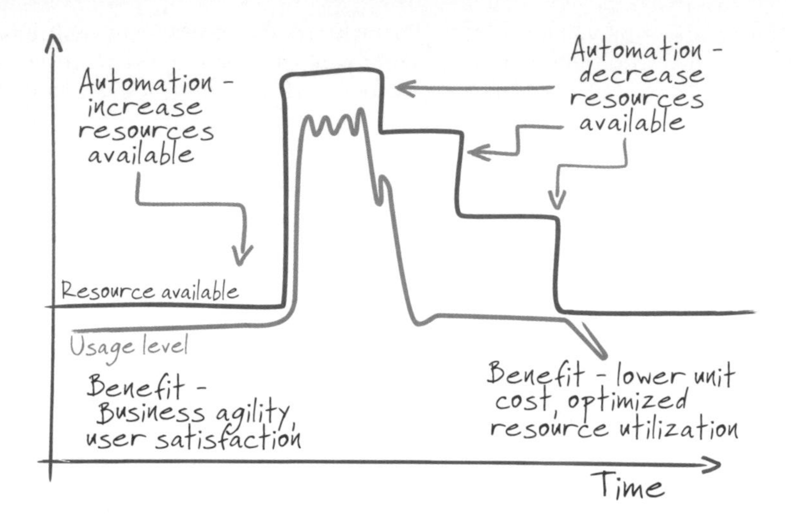

Figure 7. Automation delivers high agility and optimized resource utilization.

Some of the capabilities that are enabled by automating workload movement include:

- Lift and shift workloads from one server to another to perform routine maintenance without taking the associated services offline
- Lift and shift a workload to another server as part of incident response
- Deploy new lower cost options for backup and recovery, and HA/DR capabilities
- Maintain acceptable performance levels for high-priority workloads when usage spikes occur—for example, give a high-priority workload additional resources by moving it to another server in the pool or by moving second-tier workloads somewhere else.

Deprovisioning

The third process you will automate is the deprovisioning of unused workloads. Deprovisioning is a key component of a resource rental model. An expiration date anchors user expectations that the resource is temporary—not purchased but rented. Your service request portal should include a user-specified field that defines expiration date. Some resource requests may indicate a far-off expiration date, similar to a 99-year lease. Such requests, however, should be severely limited by policy. Other requests may indicate the actual date when the resources will no longer be needed. In any case, use expiration information to automate the appropriate end-of-life response.

Requiring users to specify expiration dates modifies their behavior in ways that directly affect overall private cloud economics. If you ask developers why they have three unused physical servers under their desks, they may reply, "In case I need them." The same goes for unused virtual servers. Developers have been conditioned to assume that it is easier to overprovision and hoard than to get approval later for additional resources if needed.

By always filling developer requests for virtual or cloud resources and taking the resources back when they are no longer being used, you can eliminate hoarding. Developers get what they need when needed, and with less effort. Fewer zombie machines litter the virtual and private cloud environments. Overall utilization rises. Unused software licenses are freed for others to use. Everyone wins.

Things to consider for automated deprovisioning:

- Automate notice to users and admins at a set period of time before expiration date.
- Give users the ability to easily extend rental periods. Don't require that users log into other systems to get extensions. Instead, give them a link right in the notification.
- Give users a second and even a third warning before terminating their service.
- Provide an easy means for users to back up their environment in case they need to restore service at a later date. Give users the opportunity to test restore from backup before their service is terminated.
- When a service is terminated, notify users and their managers to give positive reinforcement to their behavior. In other words "praise the renter."

In Phase 4, you will learn more about how this level of automation in the provisioning/deprovisioning process will also help to shape user behavior.

Other maintenance and support

There is a wide range of other tasks that can be automated to support an efficient private cloud environment. The activities may be similar to those in the static virtual computing environment.

Document how highly skilled resources spend their time. Determine how much of their nonstrategic efforts can be automated. Note that for lower-value tasks, automation may not have sufficient cost benefit to justify the upfront and ongoing cost of implementing it. Also consider shifting tasks to lower-skilled, entry-level workers. In addition to asking, "Can we automate this?" always ask, "Can a less skilled worker complete this task effectively and gain the opportunity to learn a new skill?"

Things to consider in automating maintenance and support activities:

- Consider automating high-effort maintenance activities not specific to private cloud strategy. These include workflow data collection, authorization, configuration drift verification, configuration reporting, remediation of known problems, and data migrations.
- Automate patching and updating. The constant barrage of software updates and fixes consumes a considerable amount of administrator time. With automation, your staff can "set it and forget it." What's more, you can pre-approve and schedule patching and updating activities to run during off hours. That means you minimize the impact on business users and eliminate the need for staff to work nights and weekends.
- Automate control processes that are especially sensitive or error prone. Document the workflows. Show how the workflows run error free and securely, and demonstrate that they are logged for audit purposes. These efforts encourage auditors to audit at the policy level and not the server level.

- Establish automatic change detection to prevent or correct configuration drift that results in out-of-compliance servers and applications. If you can automate remediation, do it, even if it has to be manually authorized.

General considerations for automation:

Some general IT automation considerations may help your private cloud automation efforts.

- **Automate standard processes.** Kick out exceptions for manual process. Then work to increase standardization and minimize the number of exceptions to reduce manual work.
- **Design for flexibility.** Don't assume automation will not change. Define mechanisms that allow you to adapt, change, add, and delete automated workflows when real-world requirements change. Take your cue from object-oriented programming and parameterize where possible by using variables that can be easily reset. For example, guided by deployment policy and pre-approval, your workflow tool may simply change 'type=test' to 'type=prod' to change IP range, filenames, and host files when moving a workload from the test to the production environment.
- **Gain experience in steps.** Small steps allow you to uncover and resolve small problems. Start with low-risk, low-impact environments (for example, development/test/QA, education labs, and internal systems) before moving into high-risk or high-impact opportunities.
- **Develop integration skills.** Workflow and run book automation tools interact through programmatic interfaces and not user interfaces. Educate key technical administrators. Understand the capabilities of the various programmatic interfaces and have a clear idea of what they can and cannot do.
- **Maintain oversight.** You may need to maintain manual oversight of tier-1 applications. For example, you may allow the deployment of a new file server without approval but require approval for an SAP server.
- **Control access.** Ensure that identity and access management controls are built into automated provisioning. This helps ensure core compliance outcomes such as functional isolation, user-specific audit logs, and functional authorization.
- **Enforce policies.** Shut down rogue machines, deprovision unauthorized licenses, remediate unacceptable configurations, and suspend suspicious users. Select the standards that best fit your organization and stick with them.
- **Document automation.** Systems and processes move faster and are harder to track and maintain in the virtual world. Thoroughly document automation routines and processes so that new and different teams have an accurate and consistent understanding of these routines and processes.
- **Treat automation like applications.** Maintain change management and version control over automation routines just as you would for application releases or operating systems. Back up regularly, monitor new releases for problems, and be prepared to rollback if new automation procedures cause problems.

- **Measure results and promote your successes.** Show business benefits in metrics that are meaningful to internal and external business customers. Also be sure to show senior management that the investment in automation and private cloud is paying off. This will help you justify investments in the future.

Re-architect the infrastructure

> *"Storage professionals are changing backup tools and processes. Networking groups are provisioning more VLANs to cope with increasing data center traffic. Security administrators are dedicating physical servers as virtual security zones. All of these changes open new opportunities for organizations to automate processes and acquire new capabilities."*
>
> —MARK BOWKER, SENIOR ANALYST, ENTERPRISE STRATEGY GROUP, INC.

If your organization is like many we've studied, you probably "jumped" into virtualization. That is, you kicked off a variety of virtualization projects that, because of their success, fueled other projects. As a result, you've kept expanding your use of virtualization. Because projects tended to be isolated from each other, the expansion wasn't coordinated with respect to aggregated impact on the infrastructure.

Now that you are deploying a private cloud computing environment, you may find that your infrastructure is not sufficient to handle the quantity of virtual servers that have already been deployed, much less support a whole new set that will be used to implement the private cloud. To remedy that, you're going to update and standardize the infrastructure to accommodate the private cloud architecture you developed during your POC in Phase 1. The infrastructure should meet the functional and technical specifications developed for the private cloud services you defined in Phase 2.

That new infrastructure will likely include:

- A mix of standalone hosts and clustered resource pools
- Processes and tools to manage resource levels
- Processes and tools to move workloads between hosts and within clusters
- The capability to quickly rebuild servers from stored images

If you're thinking, "We already went through a re-architecting effort as we expanded virtualization, but our infrastructure still isn't ready for a fully virtualized data center, let alone private cloud," don't worry. You're in good company. Even top performers we studied reported multiple attempts at re-architecting. One top performer that has now achieved a high level of virtualization and automation maturity told us, "We re-architected five times before we got it right."

As you upgrade your infrastructure, architect for flexibility and multitenancy. Remember that virtualization is about infrastructure abstraction, and that requires resources to be flexible. Think loosely coupled and federated instead of tightly coupled and integrated.

Servers

The number of VMs you can put on a given physical host depends on the requirements of the workload and the capacity of the physical host. Legacy hardware often lacks the

CPU power, memory, and I/O bandwidth to accommodate a high density of workloads. To achieve the performance you want, place VMs on higher-powered, energy-efficient servers with faster I/O, more NICs, and more memory.

The limitation for many workloads may be I/O. If your server has a two-gig CPU and a terabyte of memory but the I/O is limited to 100 MB per second, the amount of data that can traverse the backplane may be seriously restricted. As a result, queuing will occur, data will back up, and performance will degrade.

The limitation may also be memory. Your resource management strategy may include overallocating memory, but once memory is exhausted, no more VMs can be installed on that server, regardless of remaining CPU or storage capacity.

Storage

You also need to rethink your storage infrastructure and strategy with private cloud. For example, if the databases associated with a workload reside on a drive attached to a physical server, you're stuck with moving the data along with the workload. Separating the data out to a storage area network (SAN) gives you the flexibility to move workloads while leaving the data in place.

Similarly, having a consolidated library of images to pull from NAS or SAN eliminates the need to inventory and version control images on host machines, and allows managed access to golden images from multiple machines.

Note that different storage environments have different characteristics. These environments can run on SAN or NAS. During your architecture efforts in the Phase 1 POC you may have figured out which is optimal for your private cloud environment.

Network

As you begin moving workloads around in your private cloud, you may need substantially more network bandwidth. Trying to dynamically lift and shift across low-bandwidth connections leads to problems ranging from severe performance degradation to taking out complete network nodes.

Pay attention to the weakest links in your network. Your weak link may be the "last mile" that connects the user to the data center, or it may be a network connection between components of the overall system. It may also be the interconnect between the servers and the SAN. You can use dependency mapping to reveal the links involved with each workload.

Encourage your network engineers to go beyond the traditional MIOPS focus to more of a systems engineering perspective. Systems management is integrated into many routers and networking is built into many systems.

Update monitoring and alerting

> *"The next phase of server virtualization demands tighter integration and cross-functional, virtualization-aware management tools."*
>
> —MARK BOWKER, SENIOR ANALYST, ENTERPRISE STRATEGY GROUP, INC.

Even if you've optimized monitoring in a static virtual environment, that won't be sufficient you as you move toward shared resources and dynamic workloads. In a static environment, servers are provisioned to handle anticipated peak loads. Monitoring is geared toward identifying performance degradation or service disruption. Alerts trigger a service incident response. The key question is, "Which alerts should be ignored and which should result in a service desk ticket?"

In the new shared and dynamic environment, this all changes. You simply cannot use the same old tools and processes, because virtual systems, components, and requirements are fundamentally different. CPU is not real, memory is not real, I/O is not real. Resources are provisioned at a capacity that supports normal load. Monitoring is geared toward identifying conditions that warrant capacity changes. The key question is, "Should resource allocation be changed, or should workloads be moved?"

Private cloud services bring different technology types and heterogeneous platforms together. Server, storage, network, and security come together in single virtual containers. Linux, Windows, and UNIX may run on a single piece of hardware. With so many combinations possible and continually changing, monitoring the environment becomes far more complex.

> Alerts don't just trigger trouble tickets, they trigger resource allocation changes or workload movement.

To cope, IT needs individuals who have multiple domains of expertise who can take a holistic view of the infrastructure in a way that transcends network, hardware, and storage. These people need consolidated tools that provide a reliable holistic view of physical, virtual, system, network, and application performance. They also need tools that can identify conditions that trigger automated responses to orchestrate resources.

Re-optimize service management processes

> *"After you have operationalized your plans, you need to revisit them to make sure that you were correct. For example, you should be asking questions like: What is the capacity I really need? Where am I really going with this solution? How can I improve on my overall service design model based on lessons learned?"*
> —RICH MCGINTY, DIRECTOR OF IT, METLIFE

To ensure that cloud services deliver as promised, you need to update a range of service management processes. Bundled services, more automation, and dynamic management of shared workloads necessitate change in how IT is run.

Change management

Managing change in a private cloud is more important than in other environments for two key reasons. First, powerful tools make it easier and faster to do the right things than in a physical environment. But virtualization also makes it easier and faster to do the wrong things. As a result, updating change management controls is critical to gain the benefits without the risks.

Second, managing a dynamic environment with a high degree of automation requires more preplanning and pre-approval of new operational change models that are then codified and executed by workflow tools. Keep in mind that automation can do more damage, and do it faster, than any person. You need to make sure that rule-driven changes are tested and exceptions are worked out before you automate.

Automation requires more preplanning and pre-approval of new operational change models that are then codified and executed by workflow tools.

Now is a great time to revisit your change process and change controls. You need a strong working foundation of change management in your organization before you automate resource and workload changes in a private cloud. You can leverage the *Visible Ops Handbook* or other best-practices frameworks to make sure you have the necessary degree of change control in your private cloud.

Things to consider:

- **Update change models.** You need to update your change models to account for the expected changes you plan to automate. Using lift-and-shift capabilities to move all VMs to another host during planned maintenance is a great way to reduce planned downtime. But you don't want to have to go to the change advisory board and create 20 change tickets just to move 20 VMs to a different host. You can use hard data to determine which types of operational changes have low risk before you automate.
- **Automate data collection and audit.** Use tools and workflow to automate data collection for each step of a change process. Leave a trail of breadcrumbs. Use the data points to identify and eliminate process exceptions while semi-automated. Then, when fully automated, the data trail permits you to audit the process to verify that it is working and to support root cause analysis when it is not.
- **Identify boundaries for certain types of changes.** With broad use of automation, you need to flag corner cases that limit the automation. For example, resource or workload moves for financial- or patient-related applications may be limited to certain resource pools for regulatory compliance reasons. Build those limits into your automation routines.
- **Build exit ramps into all automated workflows.** Anticipate exceptions. Clearly communicate the process and the people responsible for troubleshooting automation routines.
- **Electrify the fence.** You'll need a way to definitively detect and prevent out-of-process changes. This is even more important when changes are partially or fully automated. Deploy discovery tools that are virtual aware at all layers of the computing stack.
- **Update component-level identification scheme.** Revisit your process and tools for assigning identification to various virtual components. The quality of your change records and dependency-mapping schemes are directly impacted by your choices here. Ask the following questions: Does a resource pool get a configuration item number? What about a temporary virtual machine or a host?

Incident and problem management

Automation is essential to dealing effectively with incidents and problems in a dynamic environment. Monitoring is a necessary but not sufficient part of this effort. You must also enable efficient root cause analysis to reduce the time spent in triage conference calls and meetings, to improve reaction to problems, and to reduce MTTR. Your processes and tools should allow for deep analysis and rapid troubleshooting. If you get 300 alerts from 300 VMs, you need a fast way to zero in on the cause, which may be a single failed network switch.

Things to consider:

- Reprovision instead of repair. Your private cloud comprises workloads that are built using a bill-of-material approach to assembling components. That assembly is a predictable event in terms of time and effort. It may take less effort and time to rebuild a workload to restore service than to repair it. Determine guidelines for support personnel that specify when to rebuild versus repair.
- Revamp your tier-3 problem resolution processes for virtualization. Tier 3 needs a virtualization administrator who can determine where the VM was created as well as who created it and when. This information makes it easier to determine where issues such as sprawl, governance, or licensing originated.
- Capture knowledge on recurring conditions in a content management system, a service desk, or even a shared wiki, and use it to automate remediation. The result will be faster response with no staff intervention required. For example, assume your mail server periodically runs out of mailbox space allocation. The fix is the same every time: You take the mail server offline, increase the allocation of database space for the mailboxes, and then bring the server back on line. This is a great candidate for automatic remediation.
- When you can't fully automate remediation, automate some of the legwork required to gather and analyze information. You might be able to establish a knowledge-based approach that says, "We've seen this problem before and the cause is usually one of the following three things."
- Put the knowledge base at the fingertips of support people to slash triage time. With a well-designed knowledge base, you can turn many jobs over to junior people, freeing up senior staff for high-value projects. In time, your knowledge base of known issues expands, further speeding response and increasing the ability of junior staff to deal with incidents.

Capacity Management

Capacity management in a private cloud is different than in static virtual or physical environments. To the user, the private cloud represents unlimited capacity that can be tapped instantly and scaled if needed. To the infrastructure team, however, the private cloud resources are not infinite, and are actually managed at greater normal workload density and higher utilization. Resources are expanded and contracted to maintain service levels and optimal utilization. Capacity plans are not linear, and capacity requirements frequently are not even predictable.

There are two factors to consider in capacity planning and allocation: normal usage levels and peak usage levels. For normal usage, you consolidate VMs on a single host or resource pool and allocate resources based on priority. For heavy uage, you can make additional resources available in a variety of ways. You can allocate more resources to the workload. You can move the workload to another resource pool in response to current conditions (reactive) such as a spike in web traffic; or in anticipation of expected conditions (proactive) such as end-of-month or end-of–quarter activity.

Important questions to ask with respect to near-term capacity needs include:

- What are the dependencies that impact delivery of a specific service?
- How much capacity do I have now for all components that support the service?
- How much capacity do I need for normal operations?
- Are there known peaks based on calendar, business cycle, or season?

As you expand your view to the longer term, there are additional questions you need to ask:

- When and how much capacity do I need to add over time to accommodate planned business growth?
- Does my enterprise typically experience gradual growth or are big jumps anticipated due to mergers and acquisitions?
- How might unexpected events, such as economic booms/busts, litigation, and natural disasters affect capacity requirements?

Don't forget to take a look at your request and purchase processes to confirm that they provide the flexibility you need to deliver capacity in a timely manner. You may need to prepurchase capacity to prepare for anticipated growth in business demand. This will allow you to get capacity online faster when you need it.

Backup and Recovery

Prior to virtualization, automated backup and recovery processes required hot backup (with its higher costs for hardware, power, and cooling), and daily tape backup of applications and servers. When emergencies arose, the diversion of traffic to backup and restore was cumbersome—not to mention people and time intensive.

With virtualization, backup can be automated for a fraction of the cost. Virtual server snapshots can be stored on the network and restored without having to rebuild the configurations. This eliminates the need for all those extra people, and the hardware, power, and cooling you needed in the past. It also eliminates the need for tape backups.

You will, however, need to make backup and recovery more granular than in the past, allowing for file- and block-level recovery, to meet increasingly stringent disaster recovery, high availability, and business continuity requirements. For example, previously you might have responded to a request to retrieve lost information by restoring an entire server. That same approach now might wipe out other, perhaps more critical information.

High availability/disaster recovery

Backup and recovery alone are probably not good enough for critical file servers and applications running in a virtualized environment. You should consider a replication and high-availability software solution—one that protects your physical and virtual servers, applications, and data—to simplify deployment, management, and maintenance.

A high-availability solution enables fast and easy data rewind to a known good point in time after accidental or malicious data loss or damage, or after unplanned system outages and disasters. A host solution can protect physical as well as virtual servers at the host level (all VMs installed on the host) and at the VM level (individual VMs.) Every change to the data or database is captured and can be undone. A replication solution also eliminates shared storage as a single point of failure.

Some considerations for a solution include:

- A high-availability solution should include both server- and application-level monitoring because an application may sometimes crash without a server going down.
- You should be able to choose between replicating in a continuous manner for the best protection and recovery, or in a scheduled manner as in traditional backup. This choice is especially important in bandwidth-constrained environments.
- Your replication and high-availability solution should be WAN optimized so you can deploy your replica/failover servers and storage at any remote site or in the cloud for disaster recovery purposes.
- Last but not least, any good replication and high-availability solution should include nondisruptive recovery testing, so you can schedule recurring lights-out testing of your replica/failover systems and data—all without disrupting the work environment.
- A replication and high-availability solution is also useful in migrating entire systems and applications from physical to virtual servers. With such a solution, you can speed P2V migration without disrupting the workforce or requiring people to come in nights and weekends.

Planned maintenance

In many industries and organizations, it's no longer acceptable to take down services for maintenance. In healthcare, for example, IT supports equipment, systems, and data that medical personnel need for decision-making in life-and-death situations. In financial services, trading desk operations can lose millions of dollars and risk huge financial penalties if they don't complete trades within strict timelines.

Consequently, you need to take a close look at your processes for routine and emergency maintenance. Vendor-specific tools can facilitate the lift and shift of virtual servers from one physical server to another. Lift and shift allows the staff to take a server offline to perform required maintenance without interrupting critical applications and services. Everyone wins. Users have zero downtime, and the IT staff no longer has to come in at 3:00 am on a Sunday to change a power supply.

Make sure your change management processes accommodate planned maintenance of different private cloud components. Create and test new change models for standard operational changes.

Make run book knowledge public

> *"If you want to evaluate the skills of your existing IT processes and staff, there is no brighter light you can shine on them than a private cloud initiative. Assembling a team that can assimilate information about all the moving parts, then working together to turn that understanding into solid, well-built processes and systems is what's needed to manage the magnified risks inherent in a private cloud."*
> —SCOTT VAN DEN ELZEN, SENIOR SYSTEMS ARCHITECT, IP SERVICES

Your organization has a wealth of collective knowledge about the various activities that go into running, managing, and maintaining your IT environment. Unfortunately, that knowledge is probably in the heads of people responsible for various functions and not well documented. Most likely, no single person in IT has full visibility across an entire process or knows how to address every special circumstance that arises. The increased number of dependencies and single points of failure in a private cloud environment raise the importance of documenting information that helps people manage their various work functions.

Top performers don't keep critical knowledge private. They make critical knowledge public to enhance knowledge management and process improvement. Knowledge management helps increase the efficiency of the maintenance and support staff. It supports knowledge transfer from high-skilled senior staffers to more junior people. In addition, it enables process improvement. Overall, better automation of virtual systems, and documenting and shifting work has the potential to significantly improve staff efficiency. [19]

To capture run book knowledge for private cloud services:

- Describe the service provided at a summary level
- Make available the detailed functional and technical specifications for the service
- Provide a high-level overview of the service architecture
- Document how to start, stop, and manage applications, systems, and services
- Clarify how to handle routine maintenance tasks such as patch and upgrade
- Document known dependencies, issues/problems, and exception conditions
- Describe how to troubleshoot likely issues and resolve problems

Whether in printed or electronic form, a comprehensive run book eliminates reliance on tribal knowledge. It ensures that every task, process, and procedure is handled quickly, consistently, and correctly. And speed, consistency, and accuracy are essential for supporting the frequent and dynamic changes that occur in virtualized environments.

What you have accomplished in this phase

- Automated build and release activities that enable one-touch provisioning in response to self-service requests
- Automated response to conditions that require resource-level changes and workload moves in response to monitored conditions
- Automated deprovisioning of workloads and harvesting of assets at end of life
- Retooled infrastructure to support private cloud architecture requirements
- Improved monitoring to capture information needed to trigger automated response, focusing on service-level or application-level performance instead of infrastructure components
- Updated the range of service management processes, focusing especially on new performance and capacity management functions
- Documented operational procedures related to service architecture components to optimize the use of skilled resources

Phase 4: Align and accelerate business results

"Consolidation, virtualization, automation, utility, and market model are essential ingredients of achieving success in the cloud. Successful IT shops architect for change realizing that the underlying technology is still evolving. They develop succinct processes with IT as the service broker that mediates across the various technology paradigms."—BRYAN CINQUE, IT ARCHITECT, CISCOIT

What are you going to do?

In Phases 1 through 3 you simplified and standardized service offerings, refreshed infrastructure and tools, and automated processes to deliver private cloud services. Ideally, these initial service deployments include:

- Self-service to order and provision services on demand
- Automatic rightsizing of resources to meet changing usage levels
- Automatic lift and shift of workloads to gain access to additional resources
- Deprovisioning of resources and workloads that are no longer needed

The goal of Phase 4 is to complete the transition to IT as the preferred provider of business-optimized services. In this phase, you complete your private cloud deployment by:

- Moving all targeted workloads to private cloud resources to fully leverage the benefits of an IaaS model
- Understanding and communicating the unique mix of cost, service-quality, and agility measures that are representative of each computing environment
- Actively reshaping demand for IT resources using a rental model

Your mantra for this phase is, "Respond to drive business results."

Instead of doing things the old way, you now respond dynamically to changing conditions by reallocating resources and moving workloads to optimize service levels while minimizing cost. This shift will result in highly utilized resources that provide the deployment option with the lowest annual unit cost.

As you make the transition, you will find that you are able to more actively respond to changing business demands. Moreover, the perception of IT will shift. Instead of perceiving IT as a provider of infrastructure components, the business will see IT as a broker of business-focused, high-value services; as a strategic partner, not just a tactical necessity; and as a business asset, not just a technology cost center.

As you work through this phase, keep in mind that private cloud practices are rapidly maturing. The guidance offered in the first three phases is largely based on what is working across multiple organizations that have implemented private cloud. With the practices in this phase, there is less commonality around what organizations are doing to achieve success. The practices make sense, but you may need to tailor them more heavily to meet the requirements of your organization.

Issues and indicators

In this phase, we address the following issues:

Issue	*Narrative Example:*
IT is losing visibility and control.	"Business owners are demanding greater responsiveness. In some cases, they are bypassing IT and going to Amazon, Google, and Salesforce for what they think they need. They aren't bothering to work within IT controls or get IT approvals. Initially, going to cloud seems like a great idea. But then issues crop up and they expect IT to resolve them. Or they decide they want integration with an internal system and IT is somehow supposed to make it work. We end up chasing data for years."
Users are increasing business risk by violating policies about where assets can reside.	"Users are breaking company policies left and right by deploying assets in external clouds. Audit has ruled that this is a serious violation due to the loss of visibility of assets—especially regulated ones. IT can offer better, more secure service at a lower cost if we use a private cloud."
Business users see IT as an obstacle to success — the Department of NO.	"When the business wants something fast, IT is the last place they go. Users are now asking a very legitimate question: If Amazon can provision a development environment in 15 minutes, why can't our IT organization? Our CIO thinks we can leverage our *virtualized infrastructure* and deliver Amazon-like service at a 30 percent lower cost."
We need alternate computing resources for peak times.	"We started running out of room and power in the data center. So the business is looking for an alternative pool of compute power for peak times. But it's hard to justify the expense of using a third-party provider when our servers are underutilized."
Developers are hoarding virtual servers the same way they used to hoard physical ones.	"We built our private cloud and thought that people would stop hoarding resources. We were wrong. The same guys that used to have three unused servers under their desks now have 10 zombie VMs. We keep hearing 'No! You can't move my VM to another cluster!' Do developers have control issues or what?"
We don't have a clear-cut cloud strategy.	"Our CIO wants us to build the 'data center of the future,' but doesn't want to fund it. It's the classic champagne-taste-and-beer-budget scenario. We have done a lot with virtualization. But we don't think we can build on it to get the kind of results our CIO expects. We really need to start with a clean slate and develop a solid cloud strategy."
Everybody wants online or near-line capabilities.	"We need to offer standard services that expand and shrink to take care of the peaks and valleys of the business. We want to shift resources on demand in some cases and move workloads in others. But can we do it with the technology we have in place?"

How are you going to do it?

By taking the following actions, you'll help IT make the transition to the role of preferred provider of business-optimized services:

1. Refine the value model for each computing environment. Set cost, agility, and usage targets for each. Position the value of private cloud services as "Faster, better, cheaper" to users.
2. Actively change consumption behavior and strengthen the rental model for compute resources. Minimize the hoarding impulse by building user confidence in cloud service availability and consistency. Increase transparency of cost differentials.
3. Create a detailed, service-based costing model for different services and for each computing environment.
4. Implement metering capabilities to capture usage data.
5. Implement an allocation- or use-based showback or chargeback capability that is appropriate for your organization

6. Develop a cluster and resource management strategy. Determine general approaches for when to adjust resource, and when to move workloads.
7. Update policies that enable automated resource decisions to rightsize resources or temporarily archive workloads. Refine the art and science of determining appropriate triggers for responding to current conditions.
8. Enable tracking of *nomadic workloads* that frequently move.

Master private cloud economics

> *"An investment in private cloud makes sense if the utilization of the private cloud is at or above 50 percent. High degrees of automation and self service, a standardized catalog of services, and reverse chargeback are key to achieving higher workload density and utilization of capacity."*
>
> —RAMPRASAD KAN, CHIEF TECHNOLOGIST, WIPRO TECHNOLOGIES

Your first activity in Phase 4 is to tune up the spreadsheet and refine the business value proposition of your portfolio view of computing environments. You need a simple model that describes the cost and benefit of each environment. With that model, you and your CIO can explain your private cloud strategy to business executives and application owners in simple terms. Start with an update of your Phase 1 targeting grid of computing environments to highlight the cost, service-quality, agility, and landscape measures for each environment. Use the grid to create an elevator pitch that goes something like this:

> *"We can offer you several options. We can manage your application on a dedicated physical server for $X per year with Y service levels, and it takes Z days to set up.*
>
> *Or we can put that application on a virtual server. We'll only charge you $X per year based on how many resources are allocated, with Y service levels. And it only takes Z hours to set up.*
>
> *Or we can tailor business-optimized services in the private cloud. That's only $X per year based on actual resource usage with Y service levels. The really great thing is you can self-service provision it in about 15 minutes. And we can automatically adjust and charge for "just enough" resources as usage levels change.*
>
> *At comparable levels of resources allocated, it costs more per year in a virtual static environment than in private cloud, but you can fix the resource levels and pay for what is allocated. It costs less per year in a private cloud environment for equivalent usage, but we rightsize resources dynamically to maintain SLAs."*

This kind of pitch helps position IT as a department that is proactively deploying capabilities designed to quickly respond to changing business needs. As you continue your discussion with business and application owners, emphasize the fact that IT:

- Offers self-service provisioning to match or exceed services offered by third-party providers
- Provides services that were developed with input from business users, and that are tailored specifically to address business needs
- Includes stronger security and compliance controls than are available from public cloud providers
- Scales resources automatically to minimize disruption from changing work levels

- Offers lower annual cost per server by increasing workload density to optimize utilization without sacrificing performance and agility

Don't forget, however, that there are costs associated with the tools and automation routines that enable private cloud services. How can you offer agile services at a lower per-unit cost?

The cost efficiency of private cloud computing depends on economies of scale, higher workload density, and dynamic management of resources that ensure service levels. Optimal costs are achieved when all the resources in a pool can be allocated (or even overallocated) to specific workloads. That requires high efficiency in allocating the resources and effective strategies for responding when workloads consume all resources assigned to them.

Conceptually, utilization and agility have an inverse relationship, that is, higher utilization reduces agility. (Think rush-hour grid lock on the highway as compared to 3 AM open road driving.) In a static virtual environment, it's generally true that higher utilization translates into lower agility. In a private cloud environment, however, dynamic resource management strategies that automate response to changing usage levels allow both high utilization and high agility. Automatic response alleviates the queuing and gridlock of oversubscribed resources.

There are fixed and ongoing costs associated with deploying and maintaining the automation and tools that manage dynamic resources in a high-density computing environment. The benefits, which include lower cap-ex and op-ex, must exceed the costs of monitoring, automation, and tooling to justify moving to the private cloud. Otherwise it would make more sense to simply stock a bank of unused virtual servers so you can quickly respond to business needs.

You can use an economic model to show the cost advantage of moving to a private cloud. For example, you can create a model that highlights the footprint measures for the three computing environments —physical, virtual, and cloud — for both your current data center configuration and the configuration of the target private cloud. (See Figure 8.)

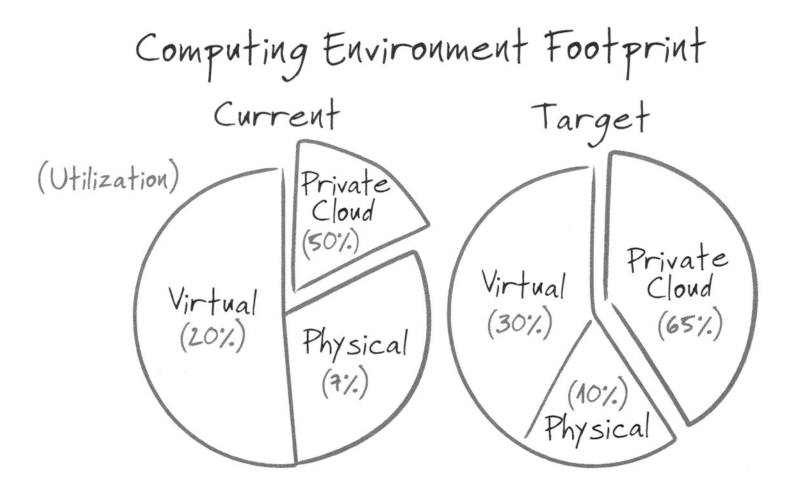

Figure 8. The overall footprint mix and utilization levels change when moving to a private cloud.

Estimates for physical resource utilization in an optimized virtual environment suggest that server, memory and NIC bandwidth can be 70 percent or higher.[20] However, there are considerable variations based on type of workload, and whether they are deployed in development, QA or production environments.[21] Other estimates suggest that 40 percent to 60 percent utilization is typical for highly virtualized environments. Some the IT executives we studied suggested that utilization of 50 percent or more is required to reduce the cost of cloud services below comparable virtual environment costs.

For cost estimates for each computing environment, many IT organizations charge back virtual servers at half the annual cost of physical support.[22] Analysis of cost comparison of private cloud and public cloud suggest that private cloud is 40 percent less expensive than public cloud for enterprises with significant IT resources already in place.[23]

You can then highlight the current percentages of total IT budget spent on each environment in the current configuration and show how that overall mix changes with private cloud. Another variation shows, for each environment, the percentage of workloads in development, test, and production, and highlights the cost differentials for each environment.

Overall, emphasize the "Faster, better, cheaper" value proposition. Highlight custom-designed services and greater business alignment in addition to cost comparison metrics.

As you create a cloud model to fit your organization, keep the following in mind:

- Agility is one of the key benefits of a private cloud. So make sure you don't sacrifice agility as you work to drive up utilization.
- Private cloud economics require high utilization to work in your favor. Make sure your service-design process is effective (build the right thing) and monitor customer satisfaction to identify drifting requirements.
- Application targeting must be accurate. Otherwise, you fill your private cloud resources with workloads that are a better fit for a virtual static or physical environment.

Reshape user behavior

> *"Success with private cloud is not an infrastructure management issue. Success comes from getting application development to feel comfortable with YOUR cloud environment. Involve users with service design efforts, and you will maximize your chance of getting it right the first time."*
>
> —STEVE GERICK, CONSULTING IT EXECUTIVE

Cloud economics suggest that the higher workload density and resource utilization of the private cloud mean you don't need as much overall capacity. In actual practice, however, the lower cost and ease of provisioning might actually increase sprawl and drive underutilization. Moreover, the perception that the private cloud has infinite capacity may result in increased overprovisioning or in using capacity as a replacement for effective workload management at the software level.

Think about it. To buy a server in a physical environment, you have to work through procurement, order the hardware, find rack space, determine power needs, set up cabling and disk storage, and go through some approval process. In private cloud, people aren't buying hardware, and costs are lower. Those factors may cause people to approve more IT projects. As a result, network and storage capacity may be getting used by things that weren't a priority before. Developers and application owners who have traditionally overprovisioned resources aren't going to change their habits unless you have a mechanism that forces them to pay attention.

All of these behaviors can diminish the benefits of private cloud. Consequently, you need to consciously manage user behavior to get the desired results with private cloud deployments. Automating processes that enable VM leases rather than purchases, ensuring consistent and predictable provisioning, setting VM lease expirations, harvesting machines and licenses, as noted in Phase 3, will help shape consumer behavior toward appropriate service consumption.

Developers and application owners aren't going to change their habits unless you have a mechanism that forces them to pay attention.

Another way to shape consumption is to thoughtfully manage cost differentials over virtual static computing environments. Many users may be willing to trade off price and control. If you charge less for private cloud (annual unit cost) than for virtual static, but you take away user control of resource levels, you may be able to get more users to select private cloud services.

Many application owners may want to specify resource commitments based on application vendor requirements. Vendor specifications and actual performance, however, may not match. Unless there is a measurement and unless people are forced to make decisions about how much compute they really need, they may hold onto underutilized virtual static servers indefinitely. If you focus on your service level commitments and discuss how your dynamic resource management strategies rightsize resources based on actual usage, application owners may be more willing to accept a variable resource environment.

Adopt service-based costing

> *"Cost of goods sold, a staple metric in manufacturing, is virtually ignored in the software world. However, with cloud deployments, the cost of services offered must be diligently tracked and optimized."*
>
> —DAVID ZNIDARSIC, VICE PRESIDENT OF TECHNOLOGY, FLEXERA SOFTWARE, INC.

The large IT organizations we studied do detailed cost modeling. Their models indicate that they can provision servers in virtual static environments at half the annual cost of physical, and provide private cloud services at a 30 percent lower cost to the business than equivalent public cloud providers.

You may want to develop a similar model. But how do you determine the cost elements for the core service package, supporting services, and different service levels you identified in your Phase 1 service design? There are a number of approaches for costing IT services. Here are some considerations to help guide your efforts:

- Stay focused on annual service costs at the unit level—per server, unit of compute, or application user—to facilitate apples-to-apples comparison.

- Consider fixed costs such as hardware, chassis, floor space, network connectivity, host operating system, and software, as well as variable costs such as the amount of resources allocated or used, facilities requirements, and other relevant costs.
- Some form of a weighted direct-spend approach may be appropriate if you have limited data. You can allocate a whole range of data center costs, including management, R&D, security, and audit, across total server count. You can add variations for resource levels per server.
- Activity-based costing can provide greater refinement of costs based on actual usage or activities associated with different services or supporting services—assuming you have access to the appropriate data.
- Multidimensional costing allocates costs on two or more dimensions such as resources allocated and usage. Increased transparency and accuracy, however, may come at the expense of a cost model that is more complex and difficult to maintain.
- You can factor resource usage patterns, such as application, network, and host, into cost estimates.
- Be sure to include application lifecycle costs such as development and test expenses and production support. These costs may vary by computing environment.
- Think of central IT as a service broker. The services of third-party providers may be components of your service offering. Or you may pass through services from other providers.

Service-based costing may require purpose-built tools for gathering data (metering), mapping physical and virtual computing assets, linking application users, and linking business services. Dependency mapping to underlying network and storage resources increases the sophistication of the solution.

Implement a chargeback strategy

> *"Private cloud breaks down barriers. Culturally an organization has to change to deliver on the benefits of cloud. Communication, cultural change, and streamlining of process touch points between functional teams is crucial for private cloud success."*
> —ERIK VESNESKI, SENIOR CONSULTANT, 4BASE TECHNOLOGY (NOW CA TECHNOLOGIES)

When studying top performers, we found a wide range of opinions on internal charging mechanisms. All top performers have modeled their service costs. However, not all of them charge back. Unlike other practices we recommend, we found little consensus on chargeback.

You should build your per-usage business model to meet the needs of your organization. Have your business stakeholders participate in the service planning and design process. Unlike external cloud providers, you have a specific market—your company—to satisfy. Make sure you are selling what your users need. And make sure your chargeback strategy fits the culture and maturity of your organization.

Some obstacles to putting chargeback into practice include unpredictable costs, internal accounting system limitations, and cultural attitudes related to permitting IT to directly charge the business. However, using cost data to highlight the differences in services and service levels is an effective way to reduce overprovisioning. Generally, top performers agree that it helps to expose costs in the service catalog and indicate the cost differences for various service options.

Showback is the strategy in which cost estimates are provided but no actual accounting is involved. You could present costs at the time of provisioning or aggregate and report them to service requestors or business units in a monthly or quarterly bill.

True chargeback may require alteration to internal accounting mechanisms. Two chargeback approaches lend themselves to private cloud:

- Allocation-based chargeback involves a flat fee per service per time period, based on resources allocated. This works for static virtual and private cloud. In private cloud, however, allocation-based charging diminishes the value to the user of getting "just enough" in a higher-density environment.
- Use-based chargeback focuses on actual usage. This approach is preferable for highlighting private cloud value. If resources are expanded to meet periods of heavy usage, user will likely want to only get charged only for what is used. However, tooling and data management to meter actual usage is a consideration.

Develop a cluster and resource management strategy

> *"Managing dynamic workloads is part of the final destination for any IT organization that hopes to get the most out of a private cloud. Yet, nothing in IT is easy. The operational processes as well as the underlying cultural and economic challenges must be addressed to gain full success."*
> —PAUL BURNS, PRESIDENT, NEOVISE

In the private cloud computing environment, managing *clusters* and resource pools is the critical core of your IT-as-a-service or resource-rental model. In Phase 3, you deployed automation to change resource levels and lift and shift workloads. The goal in this phase is to refine the automation to simultaneously achieve high utilization and agility. You will optimize automated response to conditions that may impact service levels.

A *cluster pool* is a group of two or more tightly coupled physical computers that work together to provide resources for the hosts assigned to the cluster. The private cloud model can use cluster pools in two ways:

1. If a physical host fails, another host can start all the virtual machines that were running on the failed host. This is known as *virtual machine high availability.*
2. If a workload on a host overutilizes available resources, that workload can be moved to another physical host to access additional resources. This is called *moving a workload.*

There are different tools to manage these types of moves. To be effective, the tools must integrate with overall dynamic resource management workflow and the policy engine.

A *resource pool* is a group of CPU and memory resources on a particular host. Resources are allocated from the pool to specific workloads. You manage a resource pool to:

- Limit resources for particular workloads
- Prioritize and change resources available to a particular workload
- Balance resources across workloads

By combining cluster and resource pool management techniques, you can manage high workload density in a private cloud environment while also responding to changing usage levels to maintain service level commitments. Figure 9 shows an example of the automation of cluster and resource pool management techniques.

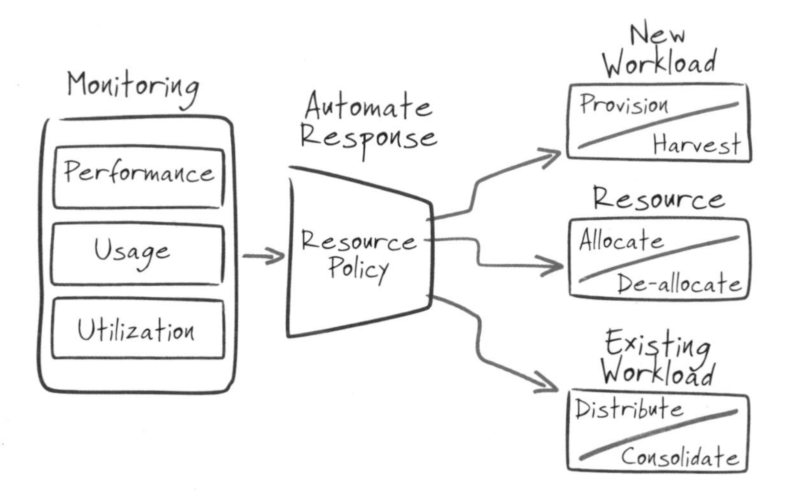

Figure 9. Resource policy controls automated response

The general approach is to target workloads on a cluster and assign resources, given a normal level of usage. Note, that is different than in a static virtual environment where resources are assigned for peak level of usage. In a private cloud, during periods of high usage, resource levels are adjusted or workloads are moved to other resource pools on a cluster. These adjustments are typically transparent to business users and application owners when their workloads are in a private cloud.

A dynamic cluster and resource management strategy should encompass several types of responses:

- Moving a high-priority workload from one host to another to access resources on a new host
- Moving a low-priority workload from one host to another to free resources for a high-priority workload that stays in place
- Consolidating workloads on some number of hosts in the cluster and turning off any unused hosts
- Keeping workloads in place and expanding the resource configuration
- Keeping workloads in place and shrinking the resource configuration

How might these responses play out in actual use cases? One example is a response policy to handle failover automatically when one host in a cluster dies. The policy would ensure that all affected VMs on that host are rebuilt on another host in the pool.

A more complex example is when an application owner requests a service with a large resource configuration. As it turns out, the actual resource usage is significantly lower than expected. An effective strategy would include a policy for automatically scaling back resources for that workload. (The policy should include notifications to the application owner so there are no surprises.)

The automated-response workflow should inform the service requestor or business owner what the usage patterns actually are, what action was or will be taken (migrate to smaller units of compute power, decommission, or migrate to larger units of compute power), and in what timeframe. Changes should be standardized and they should be determined based on policy and usage patterns. In this way, business application owners are not presented with too many decision points and, hence, do not become bottlenecks.

The management of cluster and resource pools is a new skill required to address private cloud. Achieving high utilization and agility simultaneously is part science and part art. There is a payoff in getting the balance right.

The science lies in collecting and analyzing historical and real-time workload usage data, resource commitment settings, and performance data to identify optimal resource settings.

The art is in setting resource policies and codifying triggers to react to real-time resource and performance data (including user-facing application performance) and respond appropriately to different expected conditions. If triggers are too sensitive, the frequency of automated changes will be too high. If triggers are not sensitive enough, changes may not happen fast enough and resources may be overcommitted. Either way, service levels may be compromised.

This important point bears repeating: It's the rightsizing or downsizing of resources for a particular workload after a usage subsides that maintains high utilization. Working through use cases and setting trigger levels becomes a highly skilled practice in the data center.

Refine policies that guide resource and workload changes

> *"Similar to the supply chain industry's transformation to just-in-time operations in the 1980s, moving to private cloud operations offers great benefits. But it also introduces new risks because there is much less slack in the system. It is less forgiving of errors. Therefore, process consistency, service standardization, and designed-in quality must be high."*
>
> —STEVE BELL, CO-AUTHOR OF *LEAN IT: ENABLING AND SUSTAINING YOUR LEAN TRANSFORMATION*

Policies "grow up" in Phase 4. You adjust procedures and parameters for set policies based on available mobility tools and resource pools. You reevaluate rules for effectiveness and, wherever possible, replace manual processes with automated ones. You ensure that policy updates include not only standard changes but also limitations and restrictions around licensing, software usage, and access points.

Refining resource policies is an excellent opportunity to apply lean IT principles.

Refining resource policies is an excellent opportunity to apply lean IT principles. There is risk in increasing workload density, just like there is risk in manufacturing in lowering inventory levels. Move thoughtfully and increase workload densities gradually, and refine policies based on issues encountered.

For example, you should revisit the standard images and templates you created in Phase 2 and update them to include provisions for enhancing dependency mappings related to deployed private cloud clusters and resource pools. In addition, make sure that the images and templates reflect any changes in requirements (audit or technology) that result from technology or platform decisions.

Service consumers may need to understand policies in place. Set expectations in advance to ensure that when dynamic changes occur there are no significant repercussions to the business. Figure 10 presents a few examples of documented policies.

Policy	*Standard Change*	*Action*
CPU utilization ratio is below 60%	Downsize to smaller unit of compute	Downsize automatically after 3 consecutive weeks, with notification sent to application/business owner
I/O utilization ratio is above 90%	Move workload to another cluster with lower current utilization	Move automatically (either upon impact or after reporting of similar patterns for 2 consecutive weeks) to other services on box
Storage utilization is above 85%	Send workflow request to business owner	Provide X period of time for business owner to delete/archive unused data or to create business justification for additional storage
Seasonal application peaks at 90% utilization during peak period	Migrate to larger unit of compute	Move automatically after 30 minutes of consecutive peak change during seasonal period
Seasonal application drops to 20% utilization during nonpeak times	Decommission duplicate application VMs to archive or hot backup, and migrate to smaller unit of compute based on usage patterns	Respond automatically after X days (per service level agreement)
An employee requests an external cloud test environment for a regulated application	Deny request based on employee role and regulated nature of application	Automatically provision service in private cloud environment, and inform employee that regulated applications must remain within company walls
An employee requests a test environment during peak season	Deny based on heavy resource utilization in private cloud	Automatically provision in public cloud, and inform employee of duration, chargeback, and credit payment required to proceed

Figure 10. Policies are clearly defined and documented.

Security and compliance

As you plan automated response to heavy workload conditions, you must consider security and compliance requirements. Not all workloads are equal when it comes to security. As you move workloads from one server to another, all servers involved must pass security muster.

Consider the risk and priority profile of each workload. Moving a workload to a server with the same level of security may be acceptable. Moving it to one with a lesser degree of security probably isn't. In U.S.-based healthcare, patient data can reside only on servers that comply with the Health Insurance Portability and Accountability Act (HIPAA). Moving patient data to a noncompliant server would be a serious violation of the law. Companies that operate globally often have geographic restrictions that prohibit moving a VM from a physical server in one country to one located in another country. It's essential to establish lift-and-shift rules that respect these types of restrictions, and automate their enforcement.

Failure to maintain strong security affects your audit posture. Auditors look for the right kind of controls with respect to moving workloads within a pool of like servers. They want to see that you don't move production data that requires rigorous security and tight access controls to test and development servers for which the rules are less stringent. Moving data from a tightly locked-down server to one that is more open to access could likely result in a citation. In general, to ensure compliance with internal policies and external regulations, you should keep test data on test servers, QA data on QA servers, and production data on production servers—with controls to match.

Bear in mind that many auditors are still coming up to speed on virtualization and may not fully understand the role of tools that dynamically move workloads.

Appendix B provides insight into how you can work with internal auditors to help them understand the nuances of virtualization and get them to buy into the importance of lift-and-shift tools.

Maintain visibility of nomadic workloads

As reported by IT administrators, one of the biggest mistakes made with resource pools is losing visibility and control of nomadic assets (those workloads that are frequently moved from host to host). Automation can hide issues when things aren't working correctly. So it's vital to maintain control and visibility of the various workflow steps in a semi-automated or fully automated dynamic environment.

It helps to document or tag virtual machines with the types of applications and data they contain. Maintain detailed records within a configuration management system that provides the same linkage and details required of physical boxes, such as:

- The unique ID of each host, virtual machine, and cluster
- The location of virtual machines
- The software, patches, operating system, and other configuration items that comprise the workload
- Special provisions or dependency maps, such as approved clusters for dynamic workload moves
- Dependency maps of other assets such as database, users, single sign-on, and access control
- History of change orders, snapshots, backups, and patches
- Results of configuration scans that detect drift

The functional and technical specifications of each primary and supporting service in the private cloud should include mandatory tracking features and logging activities. You may need additional data collection for production systems, especially those considered in scope for compliance. The tracking features and logging activities include:

- License monitoring and compliance controls to ensure thresholds, counts, and authorization are tracked
- License enforcement to remove unauthorized or redundant software installations due to VM duplication
- Audit trail on who has made what changes to a VM through its entire lifecycle
- Audit flags to identify noncompliant requests such as moving regulated data and applications to a third-party cloud

The service catalog has to be connected to the asset management system and license compliance must be strictly enforced. Gone are the days of inventory and removal of licenses prior to true up, particularly because many VMs may be offline at the time you are trying to harvest or remove unauthorized licenses. If you don't know they are there, they can and will hurt you.

What you have accomplished in this phase

- Refined a value model for each computing environment
- Set cost, agility, and usage targets for each computing environment
- Encouraged thoughtful consumption behavior to reduce hoarding, and return resources after use
- Demonstrated that access to IT service via private cloud is immediate, consistent, and predictable
- Created a detailed cost model for private cloud primary services, supporting services, and service levels
- Implemented mechanisms to measure usage and consumption
- Implemented allocation or use-based chargeback mechanism or showback mechanism, if appropriate
- Developed a cluster and resource management strategy
- Updated policies to enable automated response to address increasing usage levels
- Updated policies to enable automated paring back of resources when usage drops
- Enabled tracking of dynamic environments

Appendix A: Virtualization impact on audit and compliance

> *"Virtualization can make it easier to manage a dynamic private cloud environment. But it also introduces more failure points and makes it easier to do the wrong things. Careful assessment of security and compliance requirements should be included in every private cloud initiative. This allows you to bake your process into the architecture and shield it from public enemy number one: human error."*
> —DAN SWANSON, INFORMATION SECURITY OFFICER, LARGE HEALTHCARE IT PROVIDER

Virtualization in a shared-resource and dynamic workload environment can have a significant impact on an existing IT compliance and control strategy. It can create new risks that require new IT controls. It can also inhibit the function of existing controls that were previously implemented for processes oriented to dedicated and static servers. Furthermore, compliance and control requirements may impact deployment policies that dictate where and when virtual systems can be deployed.

However, many IT organizations have taken the head-in-the-sand approach with respect to compliance. They continue to roll out virtualization without considering the overall impact on their current processes or controls put in place to comply with security, regulatory, and business directives. This approach may work at first. But when an issue arises, such as a major exploit of a guest to host OS Attack that creates a security leak or renders a critical application inoperable, the head-in-the-sand approach falls flat.[24]

Some regulations not only carry heavy fines but require oversight by key company executives. Any issue resulting in a material discrepancy will more than likely escalate to the top executives in your company. Don't wait for an event to occur that attracts the attention of audit or the business and jeopardizes the success of your private cloud initiative. Move proactively and work with audit now.

Reach out to audit

IT audit is responsible for identifying and responding to risks that could create an issue with third parties, such as government, external auditors, and partners. Auditors are responsible for aggregating regulatory requirements; understanding IT risks and identifying systems that are in scope for those requirements; designing and monitoring IT controls designed to mitigate specific risks; and reporting status and making recommendations to executive management on the health and effectiveness of IT controls.

Talk to audit and understand what standards your company must comply with. A wide range of new laws governing personal information in healthcare, credit card processing, and other areas have increased the external mandate for compliance. Overall, there is more industry wide focus on controls and compliance. And there is greater interest in using technology to achieve continuous compliance to reduce the operational cost and burden of implementing IT controls.

Instead of viewing an audit as an obstacle to your private cloud objectives, embrace it as a critical component of a successful, business-aligned initiative. Many auditors do not understand virtualization technology and how it hinders or supports IT control objectives. Their main goal is the same as yours—to make the company successful. Use that common goal to work with them to better understand and meet their requirements when implementing virtualization and private cloud solutions.

Understand compliance risks

Virtualization is a powerful tool that can drive down costs and increase data center capabilities. But it can also introduce new compliance risks.

ITPI analysis of the impact of virtualization on IT controls revealed the common risk areas[25]:

- **Virtual machine and data sprawl**—It's very easy to copy and move virtual machines and their related applications and data. Consequently, you need stronger control of production processes to manage changes to applications and data, especially changes that may breach compliance requirements.
- **Discovery**—Many discovery tools, which may be implemented as detective controls, were designed to work with nonvirtualized systems. Virtualization, however, can mask traditional discovery targets, compounding virtual sprawl and cut- tweak-paste configuration drift issues.
- **Copy and propagate**—Replicating and moving applications within a virtual environment increases license compliance risk. Careful control of the image build process minimizes the risk of proliferating unlicensed copies of software.
- **Single point of failure**—Multiple virtual servers now rely on a single host. Well-meaning administrators can make configuration and settings changes that have serious consequences for all virtual servers and applications on that host.
- **Configuration and change compliance**—Virtualized in-scope business systems have more stringent requirements for controlling and verifying system management activities. Virtualization technology can both hinder and enhance compliance efforts depending on how it is managed.
- **Capacity and performance**—Multiple operating systems and applications tap resources from a single host machine. This improves overall utilization. At the same time, it creates the risk of exceeding host resource capacity.
- **Complexity**—Virtualization increases complexity and obscures critical dependencies. Organizational restructuring, careful documentation, and increased focus on process can help minimize risk associated with complexity.
- **Vulnerability**—The hypervisor layer introduces a new layer of technology that can be attacked. External threats can propagate within virtual environments. See Appendix B for a more specific guidance about mitigating security risks.

Consider current controls

IT already has many controls in place. Some, if not all, of them will affect your private cloud efforts. So make sure you understand the key IT risks, control objectives, and controls that are currently in place, as you build out your private cloud solution.

As one executive of a large telecommunications firm was clear to highlight, "Don't ask for executive sponsorship of a pilot project unless you are certain that you understand and are capable of addressing the ramifications of rolling the project out on a large scale." Why? If the pilot is successful, you must be prepared to pull the trigger on the larger implementation and understand the risks. A false start with a critical business application could result in delays of months or even years.

So, for example, while it is technically possible to run your healthcare electronic medical records application database in a public cloud, it may not be the best thing for the business. Before you even think about it, you need to be absolutely sure that you can answer "yes" to the following questions:

- Will the data be encrypted?
- Can you track and verify an audit trail?
- Will the data be hosted in the country of origin (as is required in some countries)?
- Is access to the data limited?
- Can you ensure that virtualization has minimal impact on performance and reporting SLAs?

Before you commit to a cloud strategy, ask for a briefing by the IT audit and control staff. Have the staff review the control objectives required for the regulations that monitor your specific industry.

By asking your audit lead the right questions, you can better determine how control requirements might affect your targeting criteria or dynamic management strategies. Questions to ask about regulations governing geography, industry, or customers include:

- Do we sell to, service, or have offices in other countries? If so, are there country-specific requirements?
- Are there industry-specific regulations that require unique IT controls?
- Are there requirements for protecting customer information such as credit card data?
- Are the financial applications and underlying IT infrastructure in scope for Sarbanes-Oxley? What is the impact on IT operations?

Questions related to general IT audit requirements include:

- What activities require audit trails?
- Are there any regulations or controls that restrict storing data outside of a given country or region?
- Does IT audit require additional technology to monitor, provide audit trails, or integrate at the system level?
- Are there workflows or approvals that should be considered?

- Are there blackout windows or time-based restrictions?
- Are there access or segregation-of-duty requirements?

Once you get a handle on the overall current control requirements, determine if they affect your private cloud strategy. For example, highly regulated applications may not be a good fit for a shared-resource environment. There may be limits to automating the movement of in-scope workloads from a specific host to another resource pool. There may be issues in having in-scope and out-of-scope applications on the same host.

Phase-by-phase audit tips

Once you have a general sense of the regulatory and IT control landscape, shift gears and meet with your IT audit lead to discuss the key competencies listed below. The discussion will help you get a sense of how these competencies might impact the IT controls plan at your organization. You may want to schedule meetings with IT audit to discuss pending changes as you implement each phase.

Phase 1—Cut through the cloud clutter

- **Target workloads**—When you categorize application and workload types to set virtualization priorities, you may need to create a new attribute for applications that are in scope for audit requirements. Changes or updates to these applications or their supporting infrastructure may require additional controls. In-scope applications probably are not the best targets for your initial efforts.
- **Integration and dependency mapping**—Increased complexity and obscured dependencies may be of interest to IT auditors. There may be new single points of failure that should receive additional risk evaluation. For example, a single host server impacts the function of multiple VMs, and SAN connections impact backup and recovery functionality.
- **Targeting criteria**—Work with audit to identify and document use cases that need to be flagged and managed as part of targeting guidelines. Are there compliance and control considerations when establishing targeting criteria? Can in-scope and out-of-scope applications run on the same host? Can credit card applications run on the same host as external web applications?
- **Host management**—Examine host management responsibilities and ask questions. Does the host management role need to be defined differently than VM administrator? Is segregation of duties required? Do you need to provide training and/or certifications as a preventative control—for example, to minimize configuration errors that might disrupt all VMs on a single host? Additionally, look at network management activities that now require the use of virtual server tools. Are there additional segregation requirements for people who perform these activities?
- **Change management**—Virtualization will have a significant impact on change controls. Make sure production changes go through standard processes. You may need new change models for common virtualization-specific scenarios, such as moving VMs to another host as automated response to increased usage. As always, ask questions. Are there additional targeting or capacity management considerations

for standard change requests? Are additional approvals needed? Do hosts and VMs get unique configuration item (CI) numbers for change tracking? What about VMs that are created and used for only short periods of time?

- **Service support**—Are there unique incident response requirements for in-scope applications or business critical systems? Make sure service support has the documentation and training needed to triage high-priority systems that are virtualized or in a shared-resource environment. Establish process and touch points to escalate to virtualization specialists.
- **Asset/inventory reporting**—Understand what recordkeeping and approval workflows must be in place to control software licensing. Understand the controls in place to verify asset accounting, especially software licenses. Discuss with your IT audit lead the mechanisms by which virtualization tools can be used to copy and paste server images, including operating system, application, middleware, and database licenses. Do you need new IT controls to prevent the proliferation of unauthorized licenses? A common mistake that often results in license violation is inadvertent cloning of VM images.

Phase 2—Design services, not systems

- **ID mandatory supporting services**—Are there specific supporting services that are required for in-scope applications or systems? Backup or other services may be considered as preventative or even corrective controls that are required for business-critical systems in the production environment.
- **Sever templates**—There may be specific requirements for production systems that need to be included in templates used for in scope systems. Virus or access monitoring tools may be required for all production systems. All servers deployed in the DMZ may require additional security or monitoring tools.
- **Deployment policies**—Policies that determine where and how requested services are to be deployed depend in part on compliance and control requirements. What will the requested resource be used for? Control and compliance requirements may impact the extent of attribute data that must be collected with service requests.
- **Service catalog**—The service catalog may have to indicate mandatory and supporting services required for in-scope applications. The catalog may also implement policy that prevents certain resources from being deployed outside the firewall. There may be control warnings, compliance statements, or user agreements that are presented as a click-through when services are requested.
- **Build and deploy**—Build tracking and approval workflow may be integral with IT controls. Build verification or other build audit mechanisms may also be required.
- **Process exceptions**—Measuring process deviations may be part of ongoing knowledge management. Taking critical deviations to root cause may be considered an audited corrective control.

Phase 3—Orchestrate and optimize resources

- **Deployment of resource pools**—There may be specific control requirements related to using resource pools for in-scope systems. Specific host patch levels may be required for certain applications. There may be limits as to what types of applications in-scope systems can be colocated on the same host. Rules may mandate that customer data cannot be moved out of a specific country to another available resource pool.
- **Consolidation of toolsets**—There may be tool-level controls that must be in place for both physical and virtual systems. Certain discovery tools that work well in physical systems may not work as well in virtual systems.
- **Planned maintenance**—Does moving 20 VMs to another host during planned maintenance require 20 change requests? New change models may need to be developed, approved, and added to the audit checklist.
- **Capacity management**—Virtualization management tools allow host resources to be allocated to different virtual machines. Resources can be allocated beyond 100 percent. Workloads can be prioritized. However, you must consider the compliance, audit, and control impact of new capabilities.
- **Backup and recovery**—Virtualization offers new tools for backup and recovery. Are controls needed or should limits be placed on how system images are stored or version controlled? Are storage-related controls needed to ensure proper function if recovery of in-scope systems depends on SAN or NAS? Do storage maintenance activities need to be audited at this time?
- **Change management**—Virtualization makes sound change management practices more important than ever. Change tracking and targeting controls may need to be updated to account for the new mobility enabled by virtualization.
- **Monitoring and response**—Monitoring tools may identify conditions that result in resource moves or changes. If in-scope systems are involved, do the monitoring tools need to be audited? Does IT audit need to conduct real-time tests of monitor and response as a control?
- **Automation**—Higher levels of automation create opportunities to deploy continuous compliance strategies. With automation, policies that drive automatic workflow and decisions can be audited instead of individual machines.
- **Nomadic workloads**—Overall, mobile workloads pose a special control challenge. Change approval and tracking, CI identification schemes, discovery tools, and automation workflow all may need to be reviewed as part of IT control assessment. Workload movement without proper controls can quickly create sprawl and stall.

Phase 4—Align and accelerate business results

- **Service design**—Carefully consider the impact of moving in-scope applications from host to host and from host to cluster and back. The type of workload (for example, customer or data), business priority, patch level, and other factors may limit the mobility of systems impacted by regulatory requirements.
- **Dependencies**—The tools and processes needed to facilitate moves between and within resource pools may introduce new dependencies and points of failure. Consider access controls and other controls that may be needed with new dependent systems.
- **One-touch ordering**—Incorporate limits and controls to prevent one-touch service requests that violate control requirements.
- **Dynamic workloads**—The service catalog should identify mandatory services that track workload movement and log activities for in-scope systems.

Appendix B: Reducing private cloud security risks

As you go from initial virtualization deployments to managing dynamic workloads in shared resource pools, you need to understand the risks that did not exist in the physical or virtual static environments. The key to avoiding issues is to involve security early and often.

Visible Ops Security presents a great strategy for establishing organizational and process touch points with other functional groups within IT. It focuses primarily on identifying and addressing objectives that security, operational, and audit teams have in common. It emphasizes prevention rather than incident response.

Understand security risks

The broader adoption of virtualization in your private cloud strategy creates additional complexity and risks that you must address in your overall security plan.

Many of the security systems, such as anti-virus, patch remediation, single sign-on, monitoring, audit trail, licensing, and entitlement, need to be reassessed for their effectiveness in private cloud. An assessment should include various levels of virtualization that are being leveraged in the deployment. For example, if you do not have two-factor discovery (the ability to see inside virtual application environments), how do you know if patches are up to date, whether or not viruses are present, or whether access is granted to unauthorized users?

An independent survey by Kuppinger Cole[26] of 335 top-performing companies in Europe and the United States reveals some of the most common security risks related to virtualization:

- **Different trust levels**—Consolidating servers and applications with different trust levels on the same physical box could create audit and/or security issues.
- **Segregation of duties**—Administrative access to the hypervisor (virtual machine monitor) layer and to host administrative tools should be separated. Roles should be segregated and access should be granted based on role. Loss of separation of duties for network and security controls could result in configuration drift, improper placement of virtual machines, and/or virtual server and data sprawl.
- **Virtual data sprawl**—Lack of deployment policies and change controls can result in poorly controlled virtual machines, applications, and related data. Critical assets deployed in unsecured environments are exposed to risk. Those assets can be replicated and moved, even if original data is accounted for. The speed and ease with which assets (from operating systems to applications) can be replicated, combined with the lack of proper security measures, are cited as top security concerns by 41 percent of organizations surveyed.
- **Hypervisor vulnerability**—Malware is being created to exploit the connectivity between VMs and host operating systems. Terms such as hyper-jacking (subverting

a rogue hypervisor on a virtual server) or VM hopping (one VM gaining access to another) highlight new risks created by the virtual layer. A hypervisor attack exponentially increases risks because a single attack could authorize access to all workloads on the target host. More than 73 percent of respondents expressed concern that the far reaching privileges introduced by hypervisors could open the door to abuse.

- **Dynamic workloads**—Mobility combined with immaturity of organizational processes, tools, and skills creates additional risks. The dynamic nature of virtualization causes poorly behaving processes and systems to fail much faster than they would in the physical environment.
- **Ineffective physical controls**—Virtualization may render ineffective inherent controls that work in a physical environment. For example, physical access controls are less effective when all assets can be accessed through the network.
- **Impact on multiple layers in the architectural stack**—Virtual system images consist of combinations of operating systems, middleware, and application components. Dependency mapping of these systems is beyond the scope of traditional one-to-one mapping designs of the network stack. As a result, it is more difficult for IT to see the effectiveness of traditional security devices—firewalls, for example—in the virtual environment. What's more, many of the virtual tools provide poor overall visibility, increasing the risk of undetected attacks.

Involve the security team

To effectively manage security risk, involve the security team in all four stages of *Visible Ops Private Cloud*. Security officers (and other members of the security team) need to understand how the physical, virtual and private cloud environments differ so they can help identify areas of concern.

Solicit their input early to gain buy-in and obtain their input as you move through each phase. Use the following questions to facilitate discussions with the security team:

Segregation of duties

- Do host administrator and virtual machine administrator roles need to be separated?
- Can workloads at different trust levels be combined on a single host? Can workloads at different lifecycle stages (development, test, and production) be combined on a single host?
- How is the separation of admin functions for different trust levels achieved today in the physical environment?
- Do network admin functions that access network settings using VM admin tools need to be separated from server admin functions using the same tools?
- Are there concerns with virtualization within the firewall? What about virtual firewalls?
- How does the combination of network, operating system, and other components impact requirements for separation of duties within a group or team? Are additional approvals needed? Should policies be combined?

Security policies

- Would the proposed architecture cause the organization to be out of compliance with any current policies? Which ones? Why?
- Can the current policies around systems management (distribution, patch, inventory, drift detection) be extended or augmented to address security for the virtual environment? Can the current tools support this extension?
- Is a new policy needed for communication and traffic among VMs? Should there be policies for the virtual firewall, traffic, and monitoring?
- Can current policies be re-architected to move from physical to logical paradigms such as IP or MAC address? What about virtual machine ID, user ID, or group ID? Can policies at those levels remain in effect whether bursting in or out of the cloud? Within or across data center environments?
- Does policy for maintaining the communication layer (operating system and host) between VMs need to be established for change and other controls? Programmatically, how do you enable the current network admin team to maintain responsibility and control? Is there a need to establish separate policies for physical and virtual?
- What needs to be adapted with respect to policy for role-based access control? Who should be allowed to set workloads and parameters on workloads? Can current tools help here? What needs to be done to ensure that roles are not obscured in the virtual world?
- Do new policies need to be created to restrict or monitor usage of dynamic virtual capabilities, such as moving a workload from one physical server farm to another, cloning a virtual machine, or turning VMs up or down? What can be done at the program layer versus manual?

Tool Selection

- Do you need to acquire additional tools to monitor, inventory, track, and configure the virtual environment?
- What tool functionality must the RFI/RFP specify to comply with security mandates?

  Suggestions:
  - Audit trail and role-based restriction for hypervisor layer access
  - Two-factor discovery to report on the state inside the virtual environment
  - Workload segregation and patching based on trust level (only root or super admin access can traverse across trust environments)
  - Restricted access to VM management tools, such as for cloning, take up, take down, making copies, and moving to another physical workload or environment
  - Granular logging visibility for system admin access at root and super user level
  - Monitoring and dynamic flags to alert to unusual activity and/or unauthorized communication between VMs

— Can the tools accommodate multiple virtualization technologies and types (server, desktop, application, storage)?

— Can the tools provide accurate performance and capacity monitoring for both the physical and virtual environments to permit the establishment of acceptable thresholds and service level requirements for migrations before the migrations are approved/implemented?

Although server virtualization in the data center is today's number one priority in many organizations, other virtualization technologies, such as storage, desktop, and application virtualization, are also being implemented. These technologies should also be subjected to the process outlined in this appendix to evaluate and address their impact on your overall security strategy.

With respect to database virtualization, you may have to implement additional safeguards to limit access to the dynamic database source by external users and public cloud service providers for those databases that contain sensitive information, such as financial or health data. Ensuring the provider can offer access controls based on factors such as role is critical for cloud-based implementations.

Make it a habit to reevaluate security needs, identify trends, and adjust your plan accordingly to reduce risk. The days of implementing once and leaving it until the system is decommissioned are over now that IT is crossing the chasm from the physical static environment to the highly dynamic cloud environment.

Appendix C: Glossary of terms

Term	*Definition*
Agility	Refers to IT's responsiveness and ability to adapt to changing business needs. Automation allows IT to achieve both agility and high levels of resource utilization.
Automation	Predetermined and programmatically executed set of actions that follow a specific repeatable sequence, and are triggered by a specific condition. In the private cloud context, automation is used to provision, adjust, move, and decommission resources and/or workloads.
Build thrash	Wasted effort that results from back-and-forth exchange between development and virtualization experts. Thrash is caused by a lack of standard service offerings.
Business-optimized service	IT services that are optimized for the needs of business users. Private cloud offers the opportunity for IT to deliver business-optimized services. By comparison, many third-party cloud providers offer generic or commoditized services that are not tailored to the business.
Changing resource levels	Adding or removing CPU, memory, network bandwidth, storage, and other computing resources that are available for a workload.
Chargeback	Internal accounting or charge that results from the allocation or use of computing resources. Visibility into cost helps shape demand in a resource rental model.
Cloud computing	NIST definition: "Cloud computing is a model for enabling convenient, on-demand network access to a shared pool of configurable computing resources (e.g., networks, servers, storage, applications, and services) that can be rapidly provisioned and released with minimal management effort or service provider interaction."
Cluster	Wikipedia definition: "A group of tightly coupled computers that work together so that in many respects they can be viewed as though they are a single computer."
Cluster pool	Two or more physical machines that are assigned to a specific cluster and that provide resources for the hosts or resource pools.
Computing environment	In the private cloud context, refers to one of the types of resources available for a workload, including physical, virtual, and private cloud environments. Could also refer to a public or hybrid cloud environment.
Consolidation project	Project designed to reduce the physical footprint of computing resources. Consolidation is recognized as a significant benefit of server virtualization technology.
Core service package	Primary service definitions, including functional and technical specifications. May be shown to service requestor in a service catalog. Supplemented with supporting services and service level definition.
Cut-tweak-paste	Pejorative term that refers to the tendency of server administrators to copy existing servers, modify them, and provision them into production. Highlights the power and potential risk of virtualization technology. Suggests a less desirable action than provisioning a standard system from a golden build image.
Density	See workload density.
Deprovisioning	Removing a workload, and harvesting resources and licenses after use.
Dynamic	As in "dynamic computing environment," suggests more change, movement, and automation than found in a static environment.
Dynamic cluster and resource management	In a private cloud environment, a strategy to manage workloads in which resource levels are changed or workloads are moved in response to spikes in resource consumption.

Term	*Definition*
Hybrid cloud	Cloud computing model that combines internal private cloud resources with external public cloud resources.
Large enterprise	Organizations with IT resources at multiple locations. May support multiple business units and may have hundreds or thousands of servers.
Lift and shift	Moving a workload from one host or resource pool to another. In the cloud context, moving a workload to load balance and access more computing resources. May also be used in a static virtual environment to move a workload from one host to another during planned maintenance, or in response to service outage.
Loosely coupled	Strategy for managing sets of individually built and tested configurations and templates that are combined in a build image upon demand. Contrasts with a tightly coupled strategy in which multiple components are combined and tested together. Loosely coupled permits more flexibility.
Low touch	Approach for private cloud workflow management. Suggests less human activity and more automation. Considered more reliable and less labor intensive than a high-touch approach.
Monitor and detect	Using monitoring tools to detect conditions that trigger a change in resource levels, or a move of workload to access resources from another resource pool. Prerequisite for dynamic cluster and resource management.
Nomadic workload	Alternative term for dynamic workload. Workload that is moved as part of an overall strategy to actively manage resource levels to optimize utilization.
Over-the-cubical-wall communication	Informal channel of communication that typically isn't documented. Hampers efficiency and process improvement in large organizations that are geographically dispersed or functionally siloed.
Physical	A computing environment that does not utilize server virtualization. May access virtualized network and storage resources.
Private cloud	A computing environment that is highly virtualized and characterized by shared resource pools and dynamic cluster and resource management. Typically deployed internally at a single company.
Private knowledge	Knowledge or expertise that is in a person's head instead of documented and shared with other people.
Public cloud	Refers to cloud computing resources that are not specifically designed for a single organization. Multiple customers may share workloads on a particular host or cluster.
Public knowledge	Knowledge or expertise that is documented and disseminated widely to facilitate knowledge sharing, increase efficiency, and foster process improvement.
Resource rental model	Overall resource conservation strategy that changes IT supply allocation and modifies demand behavior. IT resources are shared among different users and business units, provisioned and consumed temporarily, and returned to resource pools when no longer used.
Resource pool	A set of resources that is available for multiple workloads. The term is sometimes used in different ways by different vendors.
Rightsize	Active management of resource levels to provision just enough resources as required for current usage levels. Includes increasing resources available to a workload to maintain service levels during a usage spike. Also includes reducing resources after the usage spike ends to free resources for other workloads.
Run thrash	Wasted effort that results from back-and-forth exchange between virtualization experts and operations support. Caused by weak process, poor documentation, and lack of standardized builds.
Server as fuse	Concept that suggests server configurations are standardized to the point where when one fails, it is easier to figuratively pull out and replace the server than it is to repair it. Enables a support strategy of rebuild instead of repair.

Term	*Definition*
Server as library book	Concept that suggests a server is a resource that is temporarily checked out, used, and returned when done. Alternative expression for resource rental.
Service level definition	Description of service level commitments related to core service package and supporting services. A higher service level commitment may suggest a different set of components in a build or a specific location for provisioning service to a specific location that has failover power, redundant communications, and so forth.
Shared resource pools	Used in this book as a general term that encompasses multiple workloads on highly utilized resources that are shared among users and business units. In contrast, a physical server is purchased for a specific project and has only one application running on it.
Showback	Alternative to chargeback that does not involve internal accounting. Used to communicate cost of allocation or use of computing resources that would be charged to the user if chargeback were used. Visibility of cost helps shape demand in a resource rental model.
Static	As in "static computing environment," refers to a virtualized environment in which resource levels are not adjusted to meet usage spikes. Workloads are provisioned and resources allocated to handle peak usage levels. Results in lower overall density and utilization.
Supporting service offerings	Functional and technical specifications for backup, HA/DR, support priority, maintenance windows, security, firewall, and network configuration, which may be mandatory or optional additions to a core service package.
Thrash	General term that suggests inefficient back-and-forth exchange between functional silos. Suggests lack of process, little documentation, and repetition of mistakes.
Utilization	Measure of the percentage of available computing resources that are being consumed. Higher utilization rates suggest lower fixed hardware costs. Higher utilization may result from higher workload density.
Virtual sprawl	Proliferation of virtual machines that may have low utilization, may be unused, or lost. Results from rapid expansion from initial ad hoc virtualization projects. Caused by lack of process, controls, and tracking of virtual assets.
Virtual static	Virtualized environment that is consolidated but resource levels are not actively managed. Workloads are moved during exceptional situations such as planned maintenance or service disruption. However, workloads and resources are not dynamically adjusted in response to usage spikes.
Virtualized infrastructure	Infrastructure that has virtualized server, network, or storage resources.
Workload	Component that encapsulates and includes the operating system, middleware, application, and data needed to run a specific application. Workloads can be moved from one host to another and maintain service, transaction, and data integrity.
Workload density	Measure of the number of workloads that are provisioned on a particular virtualized resource or host. Higher density suggests more workloads per resource and may suggest higher resource utilization levels. Cost savings related to increased density are often underestimated.
Zombie virtual machine	A workload that hasn't been used since initial deployment. Also known as a ghost machine. Without effective controls, virtual sprawl may occur, resulting in a large number of zombie VMs.

Endnotes

Introduction

1. Kurt Milne, "Server virtualization maturity study," IT Process Institute, 2009. Study of data from 323 IT organizations. Correlated the use of over 45 virtualization management practices with 19 performance measures. Found that use of practices and performance varied based on virtualization objectives. Study recommends 11 practices for server consolidation; 25 practices for high availability and disaster recovery; 12 practices for managing dynamic workloads.

2. David Floyer, "Private cloud is more cost effective than public cloud for organizations over $1B," Wikibon.org, December 13, 2010. Including all related costs (people, hardware, software, facilities), suggests annual cost per seat for Tier 3 and Tier 4 applications is $2,878 in public cloud, and $1,698" for private cloud. Private cloud is 41 percent lower annual cost.

3. Mary Johnston Turner, "Worldwide cloud systems management software 2010-2015 forecast and trends," IDC Market Analysis, January 2011, #226682, p. 4. When North American enterprise and midmarket IT decision makers were asked about how extensive their private cloud implementations will be by 2013, about one-third believe 50 percent or more of their workloads will be supported by private cloud environments; slightly less than half expect to be engaging in pilots, lab, or limited production use; and roughly one-fourth do not expect to be using private cloud architecture at all.

4. "Reducing Operational Expense (OpEx) with Virtualization and Virtual Systems Management," EMA, November, 2009, p. 3. The use of server virtualization increases application uptime. Average uptime for virtual environments is 99.5 percent (219 minutes downtime per month) as compared to 99.3 percent (306 minutes downtime per month) for applications deployed in dedicated physical server environment. Virtualized workloads increase application uptime by 87 minutes per month on average, and to reduce mean time to resolution (MTTR) by 67 percent or 161 minutes per outage.

5. "Business Value of Virtualization: Realizing Benefits of Integrated Solutions," IDC, 2008. Organizations that widely adopt virtualization (over 25 percent of servers virtualized) can achieve 40 percent to 60 percent or higher capacity utilization.

6. Mary Johnston Turner, "Worldwide cloud systems management software 2010-2015 forecast and trends," IDC Market Analysis, January 2011, #226682, p. 4. A third of IT decision makers polled believe 50 percent or more of their workloads will be supported by private cloud environments by 2013.

7. "Best practices in virtual system management (VSM): Market opportunities for virtualization and management vendors," EMA, January 2009, p. 4. Top 15 percent of 153 organizations surveyed reported an average physical CPU utilization of 70 percent or higher, memory utilization of 80 percent or higher, and physical NIC (bandwidth) utilization of 70 percent or higher. IT is assumed that the same or greater utilization is possible in private cloud where multiple strategies are used to increase workload density and optimize utilization.

8. "Business Value of Virtualization: Realizing Benefits of Integrated Solutions," IDC, 2008, p. 5. The average number of servers per administrator increases from 17 in non-virtualized datacenters, to 30 in datacenters with broad virtualization adoption. IDC research suggests the ratio can improve 75 percent or more with top performers reaching 300+ servers per administrator.

9. "Best practices in virtual system management (VSM): Market opportunities for virtualization and management vendors," EMA, January 2009, p. 36. In a best-case scenario, going from a below average performer in a physical environment to a best performer in a virtual environment, provisioning a virtual system is up to 240 times faster than provisioning a physical system, going from 5 days or more, down to less than 30 minutes.

10. Kurt Milne, "Server virtualization maturity study," IT Process Institute, 2009. The percentage of changes that met functional objectives, were completed during planned time, and actions exactly followed build instruction is 16 percent higher for organizations aggressively deploying virtualization in the production environment as compared to organizations not using virtualization in production.

11. "Business Value of Virtualization: Realizing Benefits of Integrated Solutions," IDC, 2008. The average number of servers per administrator increases from 17 in non-virtualized datacenters, to 30 in datacenters with broad virtualization adoption. IDC research suggests the ratio can improve 75 percent or more with top performers reaching 300+ servers per administrator.

12. "Reducing Operational Expense (OpEx) with Virtualization and Virtual Systems Management," EMA, November, 2009, p. 3. New systems to be deployed up to 240 times faster, and new applications up to 96 times faster, saving almost $2000 in wage costs alone per deployment.

Phase 1

13 Mary Johnston Turner, "Worldwide cloud systems management software 2010-2015 forecast and trends," IDC Market Analysis, January 2011, #226682, p. 4. A third of IT decision makers polled believe 50 percent or more of their workloads will be supported by private cloud environments by 2013.

14 Kurt Milne, "Strategic Alignment Performance Study," IT Process Institute, September, 2008. This ITPI study of 269 IT organizations found that, on average, 65 percent of total annual capital and operating expense is spent managing systems already in place. In IT organizations focused primarily on providing utility information technology services, only 28 percent of total budget is available for new projects. However, those organizations enabling revenue-generating products and services have 43 percent of budget allocated to new projects

Phase 2

15 Kurt Milne, "Server virtualization maturity study," IT Process Institute, 2009. Virtualization can reduce the impact of planned maintenance by moving applications to other servers. 72 percent of study participants are aggressively virtualizing production servers. Of those, 58 percent had at one point paused adoption to improve operating procedures, and 64 percent are now comfortable virtualizing business critical systems.

Phase 3

16 "Best practices in virtual system management (VSM): Market opportunities for virtualization and management vendors," EMA, January 2009, p. 36. In a best-case scenario, going from a below average performer in a physical environment to a best performer in a virtual environment, provisioning a virtual system is up to 240 times faster than provisioning a physical system, going from 5 days or more, down to less than 30 minutes.

17 "Business Value of Virtualization: Realizing Benefits of Integrated Solutions," IDC ,2008, p. 2. Modeled ranges of utilization include 0-10 percent physical, 20 percent - 40 percent static virtualization without dynamic management practices, 40 percent - 60 percent for those using resource and workload automation. Those study participants with private cloud deployments indicate need to achieve greater than 60 percent.

18 Mark Bowker, Jon Oltsik, "The evolution of server virtualization," ESG Research, November, 2010, 2008, p. 17. Based on 463 survey responses, twenty-four months from now, nearly one-third of organizations (31 percent) expect to host at least 25 virtual machines per physical server. These numbers may be skewed by server virtualization usage in test and development where virtual to physical server rations tend to be much higher than in production environments.

19 "Best practices in virtual system management (VSM): Market opportunities for virtualization and management vendors," EMA, January, 2009, p. 28. Each additional VM costs the best performers around $452 in additional administration staff costs, for above average performers it adds $881, and for below average performers it adds a disturbing $3770 per VM.

Phase 4

20 "ibid, p. 4. Top 15 percent of 153 organizations surveyed reported an average physical CPU utilization of 70 percent or higher, memory utilization of 80 percent or higher, and physical NIC (bandwidth) utilization of 70 percent or higher. IT is assumed that the same or greater utilization is possible in private cloud where multiple strategies are used to increase workload density and optimize utilization.

21 "Business Value of Virtualization: Realizing Benefits of Integrated Solutions," IDC ,2008, p. 2. Modeled ranges of utilization include 0-10 percent physical, 20 percent - 40 percent static virtualization without dynamic management practices, 40 percent - 60 percent for those using resource and workload automation. Those study participants with private cloud deployments indicate need to achieve greater than 60 percent.

22 Kurt Milne, "IT value transformation roadmap: Executive communications best practices", 2010. Multiple companies interviewed for VMware customer journey study indicated that they charge virtual servers at half the annual cost of physical servers.

23 David Floyer, "Private cloud is more cost effective than public cloud for organizations over $1B," Wikibon.org, December 13, 2010. Including all related costs (people, hardware, software, facilities), suggests annual cost per seat for Tier 3 and Tier 4 applications is $2,878 in public cloud, and $1,698" for private cloud. Private cloud is 41 percent lower annual cost.

Appendix A

24 Kelly Jackson Higgins, " Hacking Tool Lets A VM Break Out And Attack Its Host," Darkreading, June, 2009.

25 Kurt Milne, "Server virtualization maturity study," IT Process Institute, 2009, p. 6. A number of principles risks were identified during interviews with 12 IT executives about how IT management practices change with server virtualization of business critical systems.

Appendix B

26 Martin Kuppinger, "Virtualization Security, an essential prerequisite for successful virtualization," KupplingerCole, 2010.

About the IT Process Institute

The IT Process Institute (ITPI) is an independent research organization dedicated to advancing the science of IT management through independent research, benchmarking, and the development of prescriptive guidance. Our primary objective is to identify practices that improve the performance of IT organizations.

We verify the effectiveness of these best practices through a participatory approach that is:

- **Unbiased**—We are not tied to existing industry frameworks. Our obsession is, quite simply, discovering what works.
- **Data driven**—We use empirical research as the cornerstone of our products and services.
- **Results oriented**—Our guidance and prescription drive performance breakthroughs that enable IT organizations to move into the top-performer category, which we define as the top 15 percent of the organizations we study.

Our membership consists of forward-thinking corporations as well as consultants who provide expertise in IT operations, security, and IT audit. Our members are committed to improving the operating performance of IT organizations across all industries. Through our research, we uncover unique insights that boost the efficiency and effectiveness of our member organizations.

Our unique, three-part methodology enables members to achieve the highest levels of performance. The model includes:

- **Research**—We engage in the identification and study of top performers through qualitative and quantitative methods.
- **Benchmarking**—We develop tools that allow our members to compare their practices and results to the top-performing organizations.
- **Prescriptive guidance**—We deliver outcomes-oriented prescriptive guides that enable performance breakthroughs that lead to lasting change.

The institute serves as a valuable source of information for IT decision makers. Our shared-research model allows our members as well as those participating in the research to receive data about what is proven to work. Moreover, through participation, we provide opportunities for IT practitioners to help direct and shape future research to meet the anticipated requirements of their organizations.

The institute funds research and ongoing operations through a shared-cost model that encompasses the generous sponsorship of leading organizations, the retail sale of our literature, and reasonable membership fees.

The data that support the research behind the *Visible Ops Private Cloud* methodology can be accessed through our benchmarking tools. These tools cover a range of operational topics and are available to ITPI members.

Learn more about the IT Process Institute by visiting www.itpi.org